ALSO BY MATTHEW KELLY

The Rhythm of Life

THE SEVEN LEVELS
OF INTIMACY

❧❧❧

THE ART OF LOVING
AND THE JOY
OF BEING LOVED

MATTHEW KELLY

A FIRESIDE BOOK
PUBLISHED BY SIMON & SCHUSTER
NEW YORK   LONDON   TORONTO   SYDNEY

FIRESIDE
Rockefeller Center
1230 Avenue of the Americas
New York, NY 10020

Copyright © 2005 by Beacon Publishing/Matthew Kelly

This Fireside Edition 2007

FIRESIDE and colophon are registered trademarks of Simon & Schuster, Inc.

Designed by William Ruoto

For information regarding special discounts for bulk purchases,
please contact Simon & Schuster Special Sales at 1-800-456-6798
or business@simonandschuster.com.

Manufactured in the United States of America

20 19 18 17 16 15 14 13

The Library of Congress has cataloged the hardcover edition as follows:
Kelly, Matthew.
    The seven levels of intimacy : the art of loving and the joy of being
  loved / by Matthew Kelly.
        p   cm.
    1. Intimacy (Psychology) 2. Love. 3. Trust. I. Title.
    BF575.I5 K45 2005   158.2—dc22   2006275294

ISBN-13: 978-0-7432-6511-9
ISBN-10:   0-7432-6511-4
ISBN-13: 978-0-7432-6512-6 (Pbk)
ISBN-10:   0-7432-6512-2 (Pbk)

The supreme happiness in life is the conviction
that we are loved.
—Victor Hugo, *Les Misérables*

CONTENTS

༄

PROLOGUE *1*

PART ONE

CHAPTER ONE
SEX IS NOT INTIMACY *7*

CHAPTER TWO
COMMON INTERESTS ARE NOT ENOUGH *34*

CHAPTER THREE
YOU KNOW THE STORM IS COMING *50*

CHAPTER FOUR
WHAT IS DRIVING YOUR RELATIONSHIPS? *69*

CHAPTER FIVE
THE OPPOSITE OF LOVE IS NOT HATE *96*

PART TWO

CHAPTER SIX
HOW THE SEVEN LEVELS OF INTIMACY WILL CHANGE
YOUR RELATIONSHIPS . . . AND YOUR LIFE! *111*

CHAPTER SEVEN
CLICHÉS: THE FIRST LEVEL OF INTIMACY   *119*
CHAPTER EIGHT
FACTS: THE SECOND LEVEL OF INTIMACY   *131*
CHAPTER NINE
OPINIONS: THE THIRD LEVEL OF INTIMACY   *151*
CHAPTER TEN
HOPES AND DREAMS: THE FOURTH LEVEL
OF INTIMACY   *173*
CHAPTER ELEVEN
FEELINGS: THE FIFTH LEVEL OF INTIMACY *186*
CHAPTER TWELVE
FAULTS, FEARS, AND FAILURES: THE SIXTH LEVEL
OF INTIMACY   *203*
CHAPTER THIRTEEN
LEGITIMATE NEEDS: THE SEVENTH LEVEL
OF INTIMACY   *216*

PART THREE

CHAPTER FOURTEEN
TEN REASONS PEOPLE DON'T HAVE
GREAT RELATIONSHIPS   *233*
CHAPTER FIFTEEN
DESIGNING A GREAT RELATIONSHIP   *248*
CHAPTER SIXTEEN
DON'T JUST HOPE . . .   *264*

THE SEVEN LEVELS OF
INTIMACY

PROLOGUE

꩜

"Do You Know Something I Don't Know?"

David Anderson lived in Boston with his wife, Sarah, and their three children, Rachel, Shannon, and Jonah. He was a very successful businessman, and one of the rewards of his success was their summer home on Martha's Vineyard. Sarah and the kids spent the whole summer there, while David usually spent part of each weekend and always came for the first two weeks of July.

One summer a few years ago, he was driving out to the beach at the beginning of July when he made a promise to himself. For two weeks, he was going to be a loving and attentive husband and father. He would make himself totally available. He would turn off his cell phone, resist the temptation to be constantly checking his e-mail, and make himself completely available to his family and a genuine experience of vacation.

You see, David worked too much. He knew it. Everyone around him knew it. When you love your work, that's one of the dangers. When you rely on your work too much for your identity, that's one of the pitfalls. From time to time, David felt guilty about how much he worked, but he managed to brush the guilt aside by making the excuse that it was necessary. Sometimes he overcame his feeling of guilt by calling to mind the many privileges and opportunities that his wife and children were able to enjoy because he worked so hard.

Did the rationalizations succeed? Only temporarily. But this vacation was going to be different. David was going to be attentive and available.

The idea had come to him in his car, as he listened to a CD that a friend had given him. People were always giving him books to read and tapes to listen to, and the gifts always made him cringe, because he knew the giver would ask his opinion the next time their paths crossed. But for some reason, he had popped this CD in as he drove out of his garage this day.

The speaker was discussing dynamic relationships; feeling a little uncomfortable, David was about to turn it off when something the man said struck him: "Love is a choice. Love is an act of the will," he said. "You can choose to love."

At that moment, David admitted to himself that as a husband he had been selfish, and that the love between him and Sarah had been dulled by his selfishness, by his insensitivity, by his unavailability. This self-centeredness manifested itself mostly in small ways. He insisted they watch whatever he wanted to watch on television. He made Sarah feel small for always being late. He constantly put his work before the needs of his family. He would take newspapers to work knowing that Sarah wanted to read them, and that he would be unlikely to have time to do so during his busy day. He was constantly saying "Some other time" to his children, "Not now" to his wife. But for two weeks all that was going to change. And so it did.

From the moment David walked through the door, kissed his wife, and said, "You look really good in that new sweater. That's a great color for you," Sarah was taken aback, surprised, even a little perplexed. Her first reaction was to wonder if he was having a dig at her for buying more clothes, but when he smiled and asked her, "What have I missed?" the genuine compliment settled in and felt wonderful.

After battling the traffic to get to the vacation house, David just wanted to sit down and relax, but Sarah suggested a walk on the beach. David began to refuse, but then thought better of it: "Sarah has been out here all week alone with the children, and now she just wants to be alone with me." So they walked on the beach hand in hand, while the children flew their kites.

The next morning, Sarah almost fell out of bed when he brought her breakfast in bed. Admittedly, David had woken their daughter Rachel to help him pull that one off, but it was extraordinary nonetheless. Over breakfast he told her about a dream he had had that night, and then he asked, "What would you like to do today?"

Sarah couldn't remember the last time he had asked her that.

"Don't you have work to do?" she countered.

"No," he said. "We can do anything you want."

Over and over throughout the day David said to himself, "Love is a choice. Love is a choice. Love is a choice."

And so it went. For two weeks they relaxed, they were happy. It was a dream vacation. Two weeks without the constant harassment of cell phone calls and e-mail; they visited the maritime museum, even though David hates museums; he allowed the kids to eat ice cream whenever they wanted; he even managed to hold his tongue when Sarah's getting ready made them late for his best friend's birthday dinner.

"Did Dad win something?" their daughter Shannon asked her mother one day. Sarah laughed, but she had been wondering herself what had come over her husband.

After lunch on the last day, David excused himself and walked the beach alone. He thought about the promise he had made to himself driving out two weeks earlier, and now made a new promise to keep choosing love when they got home.

That night as he and Sarah were preparing for bed, Sarah suddenly stopped and looked at David with the saddest expression he'd ever seen come across her face.

David panicked. "What's the matter?"

"Do you know something I don't know?" she asked.

"What do you mean?"

Sarah said, "The check-up I had a few weeks ago . . . Did Dr. Lewis tell you something about me? Dave, you've been so good to me. Am I dying?"

David's eyes filled with tears. Wrapping her in his arms and holding her tight, he said, "No, honey. You're not dying. I'm just starting to live!"

PART ONE

CHAPTER ONE

꙰

SEX IS NOT INTIMACY

THE SEX MYTH

Sex is not intimacy. It can be a part of intimacy, no question. But sex doesn't equal intimacy. It doesn't come with a guarantee of intimacy. Sex isn't absolutely necessary for intimacy. And yet, almost every reference to intimacy in modern popular culture is a reference to sex. If we are ever to truly experience intimacy, we must first move beyond the pubescent notion that sex and intimacy are synonymous.

Intimacy is the one thing that a person cannot live happily without. Think about it. Who are the happiest people you know, the people who are truly thriving? Do they just have sex, or do they have intimacy? They have intimacy, don't they? They might have sex, too, but the foundation of their lives is an authentic experience of intimacy. They have people they can share their lives with. They have a genuine interest in the people around them. They have great relationships.

We can live happily without new cars and designer clothes; we can live and thrive without our dream homes; we can live without vacationing in all the right places—but we cannot live happily without intimacy. Intimacy is one of our legitimate needs and a prerequisite for happiness. You can survive without intimacy, but you cannot thrive without it.

Human beings yearn above all else for intimacy. We desire happiness, and sometimes we confuse this desire for happiness with a desire for pleasure and possessions. But once we have experienced the pleasure or attained the possessions, we are still left wanting. Wanting what? Intimacy. Our desire for happiness is ultimately a desire for intimacy. If we have intimacy we can go without an awful lot and still be happy. Without intimacy, all the riches of the world cannot satisfy our hungry hearts. Until we experience intimacy, our hearts remain restless, irritable, and discontented.

WHAT IS INTIMACY?

Life is a self-revelation. It's about revealing yourself. Every day, in a thousand ways, we reveal ourselves to the people around us and to the world. Everything we say and do reveals something about who we are. Even the things we don't say and the things we don't do tell others something about us. Life is about sharing ourselves with humanity at this moment in history.

Relationships are also a process of self-revelation. But far too often we spend our time and energy hiding our true selves from each other in relationships. This is where we encounter the great paradox that surrounds our struggle for intimacy. The entire human experience is a quest for harmony amid opposing forces, and our quest for intimacy is no different.

We yearn for intimacy, but we avoid it. We want it badly, but we run from it. At some deep level, we sense that we have a profound need for intimacy, but we are also afraid to go there. Why? We avoid intimacy because having intimacy means exposing our secrets. Being intimate means sharing the secrets of our hearts, minds, and souls with another fragile and imperfect human being. Intimacy requires that we allow another person to discover what moves us, what inspires us, what drives us, what eats at us, what we are running toward, what we are running from, what silent self-destructive enemies lie within us, and what wild and wonderful dreams we hold in our hearts.

To be truly intimate with another person is to share every aspect of your *self* with that person. We have to be willing to take off our masks and let down our guard, to set aside our pretenses and to share what is shaping us and directing our lives. This is the greatest gift we can give to another human being: to allow him or her to simply see us for who we are, with our strengths and weaknesses, faults, failings, flaws, defects, talents, abilities, achievements, and potential.

Intimacy requires that we allow another person into our heart, mind, body, and soul. In its purest form, it is a complete and unrestrained sharing of self. Not all relationships are worthy of such a complete intimacy, but our primary relationship should be.

What is intimacy? It is the process of mutual self-revelation that inspires us to give ourselves completely to another person in the mystery we call love.

WHAT'S YOUR STORY?

You have a deep need to be known. Within each of us there is a story that wants to be told. Intimacy means sharing our story. Sharing our story helps us to remember who we are, where we have come from, and what matters most. Sharing our story keeps us sane.

Visit any mental institution and you will discover that most of the patients have forgotten their own story. They simply cannot put the yesterdays of their lives into any cohesive or structured memory. As a result they lose sight of the reference point that the past provides us in mapping our future. When we forget our story, we lose the thread of our lives, and we go mad. To varying degrees, we all forget our own stories, and to the extent that we do so we all go a little mad. Great relationships help us to remember our stories, who we are and where we have come from. And in some strange and mystical way, by remembering our stories we celebrate ourselves in a very healthy way. What's your story? What's your family's story? What is the story of your relationship?

It fascinates me that if you ask a couple at their rehearsal dinner to tell their story—how and when they met, when and where the proposal took place, and so on—there is a passion and enthusiasm in the telling of the story. But as the years pass, the reply to the question "How did you meet?" becomes a three-word answer, "In the library," "On a plane," "At a bar." This is a classic example of how, over time, we forget our story or become immune to its *power*.

Only by sharing our story with another will we ever feel uniquely known. Otherwise, and I assure you it happens every day, we can pass through this life and on to the next without anyone ever really knowing us. Imagine that. Imagine living your whole life and never being really known by anybody.

We also have a great need to share the story of our relationships. Just as a person who forgets his story goes insane, so does a couple who forget their story. They don't go asylum mad, but both participants in the relationship start to do crazy things that ultimately can lead to the breakdown of the relationship. Unless they can rediscover the thread of their relationship, unless they can re-member and cherish their story together again, the breakdown of their relationship inevitably leads to a breakup, or a life of quiet desperation within a relationship that has gone mad.

REALITY VERSUS ILLUSION

Relationships keep us honest. They provide the mirrors neces-sary to see and know ourselves. Isolated and alone, we can convince ourselves of all sorts of crazy things, but other people keep it real for us by drawing us out of our own imaginary worlds. They don't allow us to deceive ourselves. Other people keep us honest. Relationships help to move us out of our illusions and into reality.

I see this all the time with my seven brothers. Once a month they have something they call brothers' night. No girlfriends, no wives, no children, and no friends—just the brothers. A restaurant is selected and e-mails fly around cyberspace confirming atten-dance. It is the one night each month I most miss being away from my hometown of Sydney, Australia. But when I am there, I always marvel at the dynamic: my seven brothers and I sit around a table, talking about the comings and goings of our lives—situations at work, our relationships, family issues, and our dreams and plans.

In that forum, we offer one another the brutal honesty we all need from time to time. My brothers and I may not always get it right, but there is a sharing of ideas and opinions, and a general outspokenness that is both healthy and helpful. Now that kind of brutal honesty can become tiring on a day-to-day basis, but once a month it helps us to question ourselves in a way that is very con-structive. It keeps us honest with ourselves, by casting our illu-sions or self-deceptions out into the light. It is that brutal honesty that draws us out of our imaginary worlds and shatters our false and sanitized visions of ourselves. And while it can be uncomfortable, it creates the dynamic environment that is necessary for growth.

It is in this way that intimacy is a mirror to the real self. Conversing and interacting with a variety of people in our everyday lives brings out into the light the illusions we often create and believe about ourselves. Alone and isolated, we have an incredible ability to deceive ourselves and create images of ourselves that are one-dimensional at best. Intimacy rescues us from our make-believe worlds. This is one of the reasons we avoid intimacy. Often we would rather live in our fantasies than in the real world. Other people force us out of our imaginary worlds and provide the mirrors necessary to know ourselves.

Next time you notice that someone is doing something that particularly annoys you, step back from the situation and look a little deeper. Chances are you see something of yourself in that person. Is what annoys you something that you yourself do from time to time? Do you wish you were doing what the other person is doing? Did you use to do it? Similarly, next time you really feel the warmth of admiration rise up within you, examine yourself. Is what you admire in that person a quality that you also possess, to some greater or lesser extent? Do you wish you could celebrate that quality within yourself more?

People introduce us to ourselves. Sharing ourselves with others helps us to understand ourselves; in the process we reveal ourselves to others, but we also help them to discover themselves. Most people tend to think of themselves as fiercely independent, as if to be dependent were some great weakness and reason for shame. The reality is that we are interdependent and much more connected than most of us realize. In the twentieth century, humanity seemed preoccupied with the quest for independence. The twenty-first century will be a century of interdependence or one of tremendous human suffering. The great truth that must come into focus is that we are all in this together. Both in our individual relationships and in relations between nations, this is the idea that can most advance humanity. We are all in this together.

It is too easy to convince ourselves that we can live our lives and fulfill our destinies without the cooperation of others. In many ways, our destinies are not in our own hands—at least, not entirely. In many ways, we are not independent; we are interdependent. Independence is just one example of the illusions that prevent us from entering deeply into relationships.

Dynamic and vibrant relationships help us to surrender our illusions in favor of the often less perfect but always more fulfilling reality.

WHY ARE WE AFRAID?

The problem is, we are afraid. We are afraid to reveal ourselves, afraid to share ourselves, afraid to allow others into our hearts, minds, and souls. We are afraid to be ourselves. *We are afraid that if people really knew us they wouldn't love us.* That is the deepest of all human fears, lurking in the heart of every person. Consciously and subconsciously, we are always asking ourselves, "If they really knew me, would they still love me? Employ me? Want to hang out with me?" We desperately want to love and be loved. But we want to be loved for who we are, warts and all. And although we are afraid to reveal ourselves because of the possibility of rejection, it is only by revealing ourselves that we will ever open the possibility of truly being loved. With this fear begins the great deception. This fear gives birth to the unending pretense. We are all flawed and we all have faults. None of us is perfect. Yet all of us go about putting our best foot forward, hiding the bro-kenness, pretending that we have everything under control and that all is well.

Think about it. When you first meet someone, or are in the early stages of dating; at a job interview, or when you are being in-troduced to your partner's friends, you put your best foot forward and they put their best foot forward. Then we each wait for the real person to be revealed—revealed by life, by experiences, by the process of intimacy.

We can't be loved for who we are if we won't reveal ourselves. Unrevealed, we never experience intimacy. Unwilling to reveal our-selves, we remain always alone.

You will experience intimacy only to the extent that you are prepared to reveal yourself. We want to be loved, but we hold back thinking that our faults will be judged and used as an excuse to oust us. But if we don't reveal ourselves, in the back of our minds will always be the thought: "If he really knew me . . ." or "What would she think if she knew . . ."

We hide because we think people will love us less if they truly know us, but the opposite is true in most cases. If we are willing to take the risk and reveal ourselves for who we are, we discover that most people are relieved to know that we are human. Why? Be-cause they are human, too, and are filled with the same fear as you. In most cases, you will find that the things you thought would cause people to stop loving you actually lead them to love you more. There is something glorious about our humanity. Strong and weak, the human person is amazing. Our humanity is glorious and should be celebrated. When we reveal our struggles, we give others the courage to do the same.

The truth is, when we reveal our weaknesses people feel more at peace with us and are more likely to respond by expressing a de-sire to be there for us than by rejecting us. Everyone has a dark side, and yet everyone walks around pretending that they don't. This is the unending pretense. Intimacy requires that we be prepared to reveal our dark side, not in order to shock or hurt the other person, but so that he or she might help us battle with our inner demons.

My own experience suggests that willingness to share our weakness is a tremendous sign of faith, which encourages other people to let down their guard. When we share the ways we struggle with our weaknesses, we encourage people in their own struggles. And as long as we are sincerely striving to move beyond our weaknesses and become the-best-version-of-ourselves, we discover, much to our surprise, that we are more loved because of our weaknesses. We are most lovable not when we are pretending to have it all together, but in our raw and imperfect humanity.

Crazy, isn't it? We want to be loved, but we are so afraid of rejection that we would rather be loved for being someone we are not than be rejected for being who we are. Maturity comes once we learn to cherish the self. From that moment on, we would rather be rejected for who we truly are than loved for pretending to be someone we are not. That is self-esteem. It's not a feel-good thing. It's practical, it's real, and it cuts to the essence of the hardest choice we ever make: the choice to be ourselves. It is in this respect that Hugh Prather's powerful, profound, and yet disarmingly simple observation has always touched me: "Some people are going to like me and some people aren't, so I might as well be me. Then, at least, I will know that the people who like me, like me." That is what we all yearn for, to be loved for who we are. And that is why it is so important that we let go and allow ourselves to experience the self-revelation of intimacy.

LONELINESS AND ADDICTION

I f we are unwilling to overcome this fear of rejection there will always be a sense of loneliness in our lives. Loneliness comes in many forms. Some people are lonely because they simply have no contact with other human beings. Others are lonely even in a crowded room. Some people are lonely because they are single. Others are married and lonely. Others yet are lonely because they have betrayed themselves and they yearn for and miss their lost self. Loneliness seems to be one of those things that is always lurking in the background, one of life's experiences that we never conquer, something that is never overcome once and for all.

The sensation that nobody really knows us can be one of the most debilitating forms of loneliness, and is fostered by our unwillingness to reveal ourselves. The paradox that we want to be known and loved for who we are, but refuse to reveal ourselves because we are afraid of rejection, creates a tremendous loneliness in our lives.

It is here that we come full circle. We yearn for intimacy, we run from intimacy, we tell ourselves that we need to be free from emotional ties, but we end up in slavery of one sort or another.

Unwilling to participate in the rigors of intimacy, we try to fill the void created by the lack of intimacy in our lives, and thus are born our addictions. The bottomless pit that is created by the absence of intimacy demands to be fed, and if we refuse to feed it in a healthy way, we will find ourselves feeding it in ways that are self-destructive. Some try to fill the void with alcohol, others with shopping, some with drugs; others will fill it with unending series of short-term relationships, and in a culture that equates intimacy with sex an ever increasing number of people try to fill the void with sexual experiences. The result is a growing emptiness. Each of these is just a different attempt to fill the void created in our lives by a lack of genuine intimacy. All addictions are the result of trying to fill that void in an unhealthy way.

Addictions are among the most powerful self-delusions we experience. Addictions are created by self-delusions and in turn create even more self-delusions. Addiction disconnects us from reality. So, why do we gravitate toward the objects of our addictions? The reason is profoundly simple: because they change the way we think about ourselves. Our addictions pull us further and further into our self-centered imaginary worlds, while intimacy draws us out of our self-absorption and into a real experience of others, the world, and ourselves. Our addictions keep our illusions alive, and the one illusion our addictions are most faithful to is the belief that we are the center of the universe.

Genuine intimacy comes to liberate us from our loneliness, but when we run from intimacy we often find ourselves enslaved by addiction.

INTIMACY AND THE FOUR ASPECTS OF A PERSON

Intimacy is not just physical, nor is it just emotional. Intimacy is multidimensional. It mysteriously combines all four aspects of the human person: the physical; the emotional; the intellectual; and the spiritual. It is therefore important to understand intimacy as it affects and is affected by each of the four aspects of the human person.

Physical Intimacy

Physical intimacy is easy. It begins with a handshake, a smile, or a kiss on the cheek. But physical intimacy can also be easily manipulated. Good politicians know this as well as anyone; they spend their lives shaking hands and kissing babies, because they know that even the slightest of physical intimacies creates a feeling of closeness and belonging. I have noticed that those who are particularly good at engaging people during a brief encounter always use both hands in the greeting. They may shake your hand with one hand, but they will also touch you gently on the arm or the shoulder with the other. Doing so creates that extra sensation of closeness, even oneness. If such a small gesture can create a feeling of oneness, how extraordinary the oneness must be when two people engage in sexual intercourse.

This explains the bond created between a man and woman through the act of lovemaking. It also explains the pain people feel after separating from a person with whom they have been sexually active. The two have become one, and then have been torn apart. Even years later, people still experience the pain and disorientation of the separation. In a very real way through the sexual act, two become one, and uniting is significantly easier than separating. Many have the sensation of disorientation after a sexual relationship has come to an end, but they are oblivious to the cause of this disorientation. Multiple sexual partners can increase this disorientation. With each sexual encounter, we leave a piece of ourselves with the other person and this creates the sense of being pulled in different directions, torn in two pieces, which in turn produces disorientation.

So while I think it is important to stress that sex does not equal intimacy, it is also important to point out that the power of our sexuality is much more than physical. In fact, while the second half of the twentieth century would claim to have fully investigated our sexuality, I would propose that we have not even begun to understand the multidimensional impact that sex has on the human person. Our sexuality is a powerful instrument in our quest to become the-best-version-of-ourselves; we can use it, as we can so many things in this world, to further that cause or to hinder it. Life is choices.

It is also important to note that all of our relationships have a physical aspect. Even in a relationship that is completely confined to the telephone or to cyberspace, you are still experiencing the other person through your senses (speaking and listening or sitting, typing, and reading).

Some may claim that there is no physical dimension to their relationship with God, but again, while this relationship is predominantly spiritual, it has a physical aspect. Some people kneel to pray; others sit in a meditation position; some raise their hands; others walk while they perform their spiritual routines and rituals; and some prostrate themselves for prayer. Our physical bodies are the vehicles through which we experience everything in this life.

Emotional Intimacy

The second aspect of the human person is the emotional. Emotional intimacy is much harder to achieve than physical intimacy. It requires a humility and vulnerability that most of us are simply not comfortable with at first. The process of becoming intimate emotionally is therefore a slower one. Even in the best relationship, with the most genuine person, it takes time for us to be convinced that it is safe to let our guard down. And if we have been hurt or betrayed in the past, it may take longer. The labyrinth of our opinions, feelings, fears, and dreams is something we guard closely, as we should.

At the same time we shouldn't allow the fear of revealing ourselves to become our natural state. As we go through the seven levels of intimacy, we will see that even in the most secondary relationships there are ways that we can reveal ourselves without making the other person feel uncomfortable and without threatening our sense of personal self. Life is a self-revelation. Every time we encounter someone, we should reveal something about ourselves to that person. They might not even know your name, but if you smile at them and say "Thank you" or "Good morning" they will know something about you. By being polite, courteous, and friendly, you have revealed something about yourself.

Revealing ourselves in positive and healthy ways is at the core of intimacy. In the emotional realm, intimacy with self and others is driven by observation—self-observation, in the first place, knowing how certain people, situations, circumstances, and opportunities make you feel; observation of others, in the second place, opening your eyes, ears, and heart to how people respond to you. What is their body language? Are people comfortable around you? If not, what makes them uncomfortable? Is there something you should change about the way you relate to people?

Emotional intimacy cannot be isolated from the other three aspects of the human person. In a thousand ways that we have not even begun to understand, the physical, emotional, intellectual, and spiritual are interconnected.

Intellectual Intimacy

The third aspect of the human person is the intellectual. Like emotional intimacy, it takes longer to establish than physical intimacy does. The creation of intellectual intimacy requires both a variety of experiences and a number of experiences. It is established through conversation, by experiencing different cultural and political events, and in any number of ways that draw out our own personal philosophy of life.

It is important to note that while people who have similar views may establish intellectual intimacy faster at the beginning of a relationship, you need not have identical points of view on all issues to sustain a vibrant relationship. Similar views on things such as what you believe to be the purpose of a relationship are of obvious importance, and can be pivotal in enabling a relationship to grow and thrive. But holding similar views can also be detrimental to a relationship. You may agree on an issue, but your view may be biased or even erroneous. But because you both hold the same view, your bias goes unchallenged, and the narrowmindedness that caused the bias to begin with is only confirmed by your relationship.

Intellectual intimacy blossoms in a nonjudgmental environment. Different people have different ideas. Your ideas are not always right, and their ideas are not always wrong. Keeping an open mind is an important part of intellectual intimacy.

If we are to really delve into the beauty and mystery of the way people think, we must condition ourselves to look beyond the ideas themselves. Beyond the ideas themselves we can discover more about the people we love than the ideas will ever tell us. Too often, we prejudge people because of an idea they express. The secret is to look beyond the idea itself and discover what has caused a person to believe that such an idea is good, true, noble, just, or beautiful. What is most fascinating is not what people think or believe, but why they think and believe what they do.

Intellectual intimacy is much more than simply knowing what a person thinks and believes about a variety of issues or topics. It is about knowing how a person thinks—what drives, inspires, and motivates his or her ideas and opinions.

Spiritual Intimacy

The fourth aspect of the human person is the spiritual. Spiritual intimacy is the rarest and the most elusive form of intimacy. Some couples who have spiritual intimacy have virtually identical traditional religious beliefs, while other couples who enjoy this rare intimacy have tremendously different beliefs or ways of expressing their beliefs.

Spiritual intimacy begins with a respect for each other and blossoms in the idea that the lover will do everything within his or her power to help the beloved become the-best-version-of-himself or herself. It stands to reason, then, that the lover would never do anything to harm the beloved, or to cause him or her to become less than who he or she was created to be. This is the first principle of spiritual intimacy. Spiritual intimacy, while it does not demand consensus on all issues, does demand consensus on our essential purpose.

Our essential purpose is the foundation upon which we build a life filled with passion and purpose. You are here to become the-best-version-of-yourself. This essential purpose also provides the common purpose for every relationship. The first purpose of every relationship is to help each other become the-best-version-of-ourselves. It doesn't matter if the relationship is between husband and wife, parent and child, friend and neighbor, or business executive and customer. The first purpose, obligation, and responsibility of a relationship is to help each other achieve our essential purpose.

This common purpose is the foundation of spiritual intimacy. We may have investigated the physical aspect of the human person, we may have delved into the emotional and psychological aspect of the human person, and we may have a reasonable understanding of the intellectual faculties and capacities of the human person, but the make-up and potential of the spiritual aspect of the human person in many ways remains uncharted territory. The reason is that our spiritual potential is both difficult to explore and easy to neglect.

In the area of spiritual intimacy, there is one trap that we can easily fall into whether we consider ourselves spiritual people or not. In relationships, especially if we find ourselves in an extraordinary relationship, we can find ourselves exposed to a rare type of idolatry. By no means a thing of the past, idolatry occurs when we misplace our priorities. There is a natural order, to which most people are oriented: God, family, friends, work, recreation, and so on. If we find ourselves in a relationship with a person who is able to fulfill us in ways we have not previously known, the danger is to love the gift more than the giver of the gift.

Spiritual intimacy is best approached as an open-minded adventure in which we seek to discover the truth of every situation and to apply that truth as we strive to help each other become the-best-version-of-ourselves.

In a world of stereotypes and sound bites, when we speak of spirituality it is easy to conjure images of incense burning and light instrumental music playing in the background. This is to tragically overlook the real work of spirituality, which is to grow in virtue so as to achieve our essential purpose (become the-best-version-of-ourselves). The role of spirituality in relationships is to provide the tools necessary to help us grow in virtue.

Virtue makes all respectful relationships possible. Two patient people will have a better relationship than two impatient people. Two generous people will have a better relationship than two selfish people. Two forgiving people will have a better relationship than two people who choose to hold grudges and refuse to forgive. A considerate couple will have a better relationship than an inconsiderate couple. Two faithful people will always have a better relationship than two unfaithful people. Two disciplined people will always have a better relationship than two undisciplined people.

Virtue makes for great relationships.

Why? Virtue is the foundation of character. You can build your life on the foundation of virtues such as patience, kindness, humility, gentleness, forgiveness, and love. Or you can build your life on the foundation of whims, cravings, fancies, illegitimate wants, and selfish desires. The former will create a life of passion and purpose, while the later will create an irritable, restless, and discontented life.

Is virtue out of date? Only if we are no longer interested in having great relationships.

In our relationships, we have to make the same choice: to build upon a foundation of virtue, or upon a foundation of selfishness. If we choose to base our relationships upon the foundation of a common goal to become the-best-version-of-ourselves, and understand that the best way to pursue this goal is by growing in virtue, then our relationship will likely be marked with joyfulness and contentedness. On the other hand if we choose to build our relationships on our unsteady and ever shifting whims, cravings, and self-centered desires, our relationship will more than likely be marked by an irritable, restless, and discontented spirit.

Of course, if we have already started building a relationship on the shifting grounds of personal pleasure rather than the solid ground of common purpose, it may be necessary to demolish certain parts of the relationship in order to build a stronger foundation. This process is a painful one and requires an enormous discipline and commitment on the part of both people, because it is all too easy to return to our previous patterns.

Spiritual intimacy is the most rewarding form of intimacy and the hardest to achieve. Once you have tasted spiritual intimacy you will discover that physical, emotional, and intellectual intimacy, while breathtaking in their own right, do not belong in the same realm as spiritual intimacy. You will also discover that as you and your partner grow in spiritual intimacy, your experience of physical, emotional, and intellectual intimacy will also be heightened. At the core of the human person is the soul, and it yearns to be fed and nurtured.

In our quest for intimacy we must move beyond our preoccupation with the physical and understand what each of the four aspects has to contribute to our relationships. Physical intimacy is limited. But emotional, intellectual, and spiritual intimacies are limitless, and relatively unexplored. And, truth be told, if you truly wish to experience the upper reaches of physical intimacy you must first explore and develop the depths of emotional, intellectual, and spiritual intimacy.

We should pay careful attention, especially if we are just beginning a relationship, to see that we grow steadily in each of the four areas of intimacy. The danger is that we develop one type of intimacy very quickly and neglect the other forms. This imbalance creates a distortion in our relationship.

Allow me to draw this comparison as an example. Sometimes a young woman who is very beautiful learns quickly that people pay more attention to her than to others, are more willing to be of assistance, want to please her, and in many cases will give her whatever she wants—simply because she is very beautiful. At the time, the young woman thinks this is wonderful; her friends, too, may crave the attention that is being showered upon her. But in time it begins to stunt her growth in other areas. She begins to overvalue her physical appearance, becomes preoccupied with it, and begins to view reality in relation to her physical beauty. As a result, she neglects other aspects of her personal development, which over time will create a distortion in her character. The same thing can, of course, happen to a young man. The point is that each of the four aspects of a person should be nurtured equally. It is the maturity of all four that creates harmony and fulfillment for the whole person.

Another very common abuse takes place among people who consider themselves religious or spiritual. They may pursue their spirituality with reckless abandon, but neglect their physical, emotional, and intellectual aspects. The result is, again, a distortion of character.

The same thing happens in relationships. When physical intimacy is established too quickly, we may think it is wonderful, but almost immediately it begins to stunt the growth of the relationship. We begin to overvalue physical intimacy, become preoccupied with it, and begin to judge and value our relationship on the basis of physical intimacy. As a result, we neglect the nurturing of the emotional, intellectual, and spiritual aspects of the relationship, and over time that neglect will create a distortion in its very character.

Intimacy is sharing the journey to become the-best-version-of-ourselves with another person. It is a mutual self-revelation that takes place gradually, cannot be rushed, and can only be realized by the commitment of time. Most of all, it is critical that we recognize that intimacy cannot be confined merely to the physical realm, or to any one other realm. So, as we journey through the seven levels of intimacy in part two of this book, it is important for us to pay attention to the way each level of intimacy affects the physical, emotional, intellectual, and spiritual aspects of our relationships.

GETTING COMFORTABLE WITH OURSELVES

Each year I visit more than a hundred cities in the United States as part of my regular speaking schedule, and in most of those cities I will visit a high school. One of my favorite topics in that setting is choices and how they affect our lives. After a short introduction, I usually ask the students what they think the biggest choices they will make in the next fifteen years will be. They always cite the same things: which college to go to, what career to pursue, and whom to marry.

I then ask them how they are going to choose a college, a career, and a spouse. When we discuss the criteria they will use to choose a spouse, the answers usually range from "a great body" to "a lot of money" and from "common interests" to "a good sense of humor." All in all, I am amazed at how peer-driven and insecure so many young people are today, in a world where they have more opportunities than any generation before them.

Some time ago, at an all-girls' high school in Louisville, Kentucky, our discussion turned to the importance of being comfortable with ourselves. Our culture sends both young men and young women many distorting messages about how to look and act and live. I believe our culture is particularly cruel in this way toward women; the messages that are constantly being conveyed in movies, in magazines, and on television can be tremendously damaging to a young woman's psyche and sense of self.

One of the young women asked, "So, how do you learn to be comfortable with yourself?"

"You have to learn to enjoy your own company," I replied. "Before you can learn to be with someone else, you need to learn to be alone. Until you are comfortable being with yourself, you will always be afraid of being alone.

"If you are not comfortable alone, if you are not comfortable in your own company, there is a great danger you will end up hanging out with the wrong friends because you are scared to be alone . . . and, worse than that, if you don't learn to enjoy your own company, there's a good chance you will end up dating the wrong guys and marrying the wrong man because you will act out of your fear of being alone."

Girls always laugh when I say, "Once you have learned to enjoy your own company and once you are comfortable with yourself, you very quickly realize that most dates are not worth having. It is then that you discover that a hot bath and a good book are better than most dates."

What is true for these young women in high school is true for you and me also, and it goes without saying that men need to learn to be comfortable with themselves just as much as women do. The point is that the first step toward intimacy with others is intimacy with self. Until you are comfortable with yourself at each of the seven levels of intimacy, you will never go there with another person.

Being comfortable with ourselves is the beginning of this intimacy with self. So many of the things that stop us from becoming the-best-version-of-ourselves we do because we are afraid to step out of the crowd. One of the pivotal moments in a person's development takes place when he or she steps away from the crowd in order to defend or celebrate the-best-version-of-himself or herself. This stepping away from our peers and into ourselves is particularly important when it comes to relationships. Too many people end up in the wrong relationship because they are not comfortable with themselves and are scared to be alone.

The question remains: How do we learn to be comfortable with ourselves?

The first step is to consciously acknowledge the essential truth of the human condition. While the human person is wonderful

and capable of extraordinary things, we are all broken. We are imperfect. We all have faults, failings, and flaws. The defects we so
often despise are actually a wonderful part of our humanity.

The great truth that arises from our acknowledgment of the
limitations and brokenness of the human race is that while we are
each remarkably unique, we are in a very real way the same. In
essence, no man or woman is better than the next. While this truth
may become blurred by disproportionate distribution of power
and wealth, it remains one of the essential truths that govern
human interactions.

If we will allow ourselves to reflect adequately on the truth that
we all have faults and failings, we will grow more and more comfortable with ourselves, and more and more comfortable in the
company of others, be they kings or crowds.

As long as men and women from every walk of life pretend to
be so much more than they are, they will never be comfortable
with themselves. We become comfortable with ourselves only
when we acknowledge that we have strengths and weaknesses.
Most people spend their lives trying to hide their weaknesses, and
it costs them an awful lot of energy. When we humbly acknowledge our brokenness and our weaknesses, we are liberated from the
great pretense. We no longer have to spend all that energy pretending that we are someone we are not, and with our weaknesses
out in the open we are now free to work to overcome them or to
learn to live with them.

While these words fall very easily to the page and, I hope,
make sense, as with most things it is much more difficult to achieve
this disposition than it is to write about it. Returning, then, to our
question: How do we learn to be comfortable with ourselves? Only
by spending time alone. One of the arenas that all men and woman
of great achievement have learned to master is the garden of solitude. In the past I have written extensively about the classroom of

silence, but in my recent reflections I have come to realize that I have been remiss in neglecting to mention the enormous value of solitude.

It is in solitude and silence that we learn most about ourselves. In those precious moments, undisturbed by the comings and goings of the world, we are able to develop a sense of our legitimate needs, our deepest desires, and our talents and abilities. We have much to learn from silence and solitude. We have a tremendous need to step into the great classrooms of silence and solitude each day for a few moments to get reconnected with ourselves.

It may seem a little paradoxical, but the first step in achieving intimacy with others is getting comfortable with yourself.

Most people are not comfortable with themselves. I know there are many circumstances when I am not comfortable with myself, or with others. For example, I am horribly shy among strangers. I know, it sounds absurd, because I am in those settings every single day, yet they make me very uncomfortable. Once I know somebody or have been introduced I am fine, but I don't think I have introduced myself to a stranger in ten years.

Most people can't see that about me. They find the idea preposterous and tend to say things like "But you speak in front of thousands and thousands of people!" It doesn't matter. That's different. Only the people close to me become aware, over time, of this strange shyness.

As I write, it occurs to me that I will have to force myself to introduce myself to some strangers in the days and weeks ahead. Doing so will help me grow. It will help me become more comfortable with myself.

In one way or another most people are not comfortable with themselves and their discomfort can limit the way they experience intimacy.

If we are going to experience intimacy—that is, to reveal ourselves—to some extent we have to know ourselves and be comfortable with ourselves. I say "to some extent" because nobody
knows himself completely and nobody is completely comfortable
with herself. The effort to truly know yourself is a lifelong effort,
much like our quest to become the-best-version-of-ourselves!

The first step toward experiencing true intimacy is getting
comfortable with yourself and learning to enjoy your own company.

BEYOND THE MYTH

The seven levels of intimacy will help you move beyond the
myths and illusions that our modern culture sustains regarding relationships. Free from these myths and illusions, you will be
able to move into a genuine understanding and experience of intimacy in your own life. If we can move beyond our one-
dimensional physical view of intimacy, and learn to explore the
physical, emotional, intellectual, and spiritual aspects of ourselves
and each other, we will find reason to spend a whole lifetime together.

The one-dimensional view of intimacy as sex simply does not
have what it takes to sustain a relationship. And while our primary
goal in a relationship is not simply to sustain it, intimacy can only
truly be experienced in a relationship that spans many years.

Intimacy is mutual self-revelation. It is two people constantly
discovering and rediscovering each other. It is an endless process
because our personalities have an endless number of layers. Conversation, shared experiences, and simply spending time together
peel back these layers and reveal new and different aspects of our

personalities. Intimacy is also a constant rediscovering because our preferences change, our hopes and dreams change, and as a result so does the way we want to spend our days and weeks. Intimacy takes time.

If we can move beyond the myth that intimacy equals sex and learn to enjoy discovering another person in all the wonderful ways in which that is possible, then relationships have the power to bring a level of fulfillment and satisfaction that no other human activity can produce.

There is a song entitled "Faithfully" by the band Journey that speaks about life on the road as a musician, the endless hours on the bus traveling under the "midnight sun," and the separation from family and friends that such a life creates. One line has always struck me powerfully. In contrast to the challenges being on the road creates in his relationship, the performer sings, "I get the joy / Of rediscovering you." Too often, we make the monumental mistake of thinking we know a person. This assumption can stop a relationship from growing and can smother the growth of a person. It is impossible to know a person completely. And because we are constantly changing as individuals, there are constantly new facets of our personalities for those who love us to discover.

The real tragedy is that once we fool ourselves into believing we know a person, we stop discovering that person. If they do something that doesn't fit our mold for them we say, "Why did you do that? That's not like you!" The process of discovering another person in a relationship is endless. The discovering and rediscovering of each other is intimacy. It is not a task to be finished so you can move on to the next task. It is a process to be enjoyed.

You may think you know just about everything there is to know about your partner, but you will be amazed at what you are missing out on if you open yourself up to taking another look. So, from time to time, it may help to approach each other as if for the first time. In this way you will experience the joy of rediscovery.

Intimacy is not always about seeing new things. Sometimes it is about seeing what has always been before you, but in a different light or from a new perspective.

CHAPTER TWO

※

COMMON INTERESTS
ARE NOT ENOUGH

OUR INTERESTS CHANGE

Common interests aren't enough to create a dynamic relationship. They can be a part of one, certainly, but they don't guarantee the success of a relationship. Interests change. People lose interest in different things, and if the strongest bond you have with a person is your common interests, he or she might lose interest in you when his or her interests change.

Every day relationships break down and people break up. Some people end relationships because they don't feel fulfilled. Others break up when they are not growing. Some break up when they are challenged to grow and don't want to change. Others meet someone else who at that moment seems more appealing for any number of reasons. Some people end a relationship because they simply get bored. And some break up for reasons that they are either unaware of or stunningly unable to articulate.

Too often we spend too much time asking or wondering why it didn't work out. Why do friendships end? Why do people break up? These are great questions, but surely the more important question is, What keeps people together? And not just together, but together in dynamic relationships. For the primary goal of relationships is not simply to stay together. Many people succeed in staying together but have failed relationships: their relationships are surviving but not thriving.

Common interests are not enough to build a great relationship on. You may enjoy hiking together or traveling together, biking together or listening to live music together. You may share a love of movies, museums, art, animals, or any number of interests that can draw people together. But it is a mistake to think that these provide a solid foundation for a long-term relationship. In fact, common interests can very often turn out to be a false foundation, creating the illusion of a deeper relationship than was actually present.

Common interests quite simply are not enough to build a dynamic long-term relationship upon. You need a common purpose. If we are going to further our understanding of relationships, questions such as, Why do people break up? and What keeps people together? are great questions. But it is pointless to try to experience the deeper realities of relationship unless we are willing to start with the most fundamental question: What is the meaning and purpose of relationship? Any attempt to improve our understanding and deepen our experience of relationship without first thoroughly examining this question is an exercise in futility of monumental proportions.

What keeps people together in dynamic relationships? A common purpose. Why do people break up? Because they have no sense of common purpose; or they lose sight of their common purpose; or their common purpose becomes unimportant to them.

So in order to create extraordinary relationships we have to develop a common understanding of a shared purpose. But before we can understand the purpose of our relationships, we must first understand our purpose as individuals.

WHAT IS THE MEANING OF LIFE?

What is the meaning of life? What are we here for? What is the purpose of our existence? Modern popular culture proclaims directly and indirectly every day that life is merely a pleasure-seeking exercise. "If it feels good, do it" seems to be the credo. It is this same voice of popular culture that creates the confusion between sex and intimacy, between common interests and a dynamic relationship, and that perpetuates a thousand other myths and illusions that lead men and woman ever deeper into the despair of purposelessness. There is nothing more depressing than not knowing your purpose.

Our essential purpose is to become the-best-version-of-ourselves.

This one principle will bring more clarity to your life than all you have ever learned put together—and, more than that, it will help you to live and celebrate all the great wisdom you have learned in your journey so far.

Everything makes sense in relation to our essential purpose.

What makes a good friend? Well, take a blank piece of paper and jot down a list of your friends. Now go through the list and place a check next to the names of those who are helping you become the-best-version-of-yourself!

Now go back through that list and place a check next to the names of the people whom you are helping to become the-best-version-of-themselves, because that's what makes you a good friend.

What makes a good movie? Is it one that has a lot of action or a cast of Hollywood icons and celebrities? No. A good movie is one that you walk out of saying to yourself, "That movie inspired me to want to be all I can be."

What makes a good book? Is it one that has a great cover or has an interesting story line, or that is on the best-seller list? No. A good book is one that you finish thinking, "That book inspired me to become the-best-version-of-myself." (Create your own best-seller list of books that can help you achieve your essential purpose. Share the list with your friends.)

Why do we go to work? Is it just to make money? Certainly, at times, we look at work this way, but once we discover our essential purpose we begin to see that making money is the secondary value of work. The primary value of work is that when we work hard and well, paying attention to the details of our work, we develop character. Work is just another opportunity to achieve our essential purpose. Through any honest work, we have the opportunity to develop virtue, the building blocks of the-best-version-of-ourselves.

What is the meaning and purpose of marriage? Is marriage just two people living together and paying the bills together? No. The meaning and purpose of marriage is for two people to challenge and encourage each other to become the-best-version-of-themselves, and then to raise their children and educate them to become the-best-version-of-themselves.

Why is the human spirit so energized by sports? The reason is that sports are a microcosm of the human experience; they are an opportunity to have other human beings challenge us to change, to grow, to improve ourselves, and to explore our potential. We love to participate in sports and we love watching others participate, because in sports we see the human drama unfolding before us. And that drama is the quest to better ourselves, to stretch beyond our limitations, to become the-best-version-of-ourselves—to achieve our essential purpose. When I look at stadiums filled with thousands of people watching baseball, football, and basketball, I see whole generations yearning for something they have lost—their essential purpose. Devotees may argue that one sport is inherently superior to another. I prefer to think of all sports as a chance for us to have other human beings push us to excel, and in this they are all equal.

What makes a good meal? Is it just the foods you have been craving all day? No. A good meal is one that helps you become the-best-version-of-yourself.

What is good music? Music that inspires you to become the-best-version-of-yourself is good music.

Everything makes sense in relation to our essential purpose. And everything should be embraced or rejected according to how it affects our essential purpose. The things that help us become the-best-version-of-ourselves should be embraced and celebrated. Those things that stop us from becoming our best selves should be avoided and rejected. Life is choices. In every moment the only question we need to ask ourselves is, Which of the options before me will help me become the-best-version-of-myself? This one question summarizes a worldview, a philosophy of life, and provides the ultimate decision-making tool.

In a world where so little makes sense, understanding our essential purpose makes sense of everything. In a world of clutter and confusion, understanding our essential purpose brings a startling clarity to the moments of our everyday lives. In a world filled with experts and their contradictory theories, understanding our essential purpose helps us to listen once again to the quiet voice within.

Modern popular culture is very skeptical of, even cynical about, the idea that our existence might have some common and universal meaning. The phrase "the meaning of life" has almost become a negative cliché and is used tongue-in-cheek more often than it is to imply serious examination of the purpose of our existence. But without a clear understanding of our essential purpose, our lives become aimless, rootless, and adrift.

Your essential purpose is to become the-best-version-of-yourself. Plant that one idea at the center of your life. Base every decision upon your essential purpose. Make every choice with your essential purpose in mind. Place this one idea at the center of your inner dialogue and you will very quickly understand why ideas change the world.

Everything makes sense in relation to our essential purpose, especially relationships.

What Is the Purpose of a Relationship?

R elationships only make sense in relation to the overall purpose of your life. If we are unable to establish this essential purpose for our lives, then we will find it very difficult to bring focus to our relationships. But now that we have established our essential purpose, it is much easier to understand the meaning and purpose of our relationships. The purpose of relationships is for you to help others become the-best-version-of-themselves, and for others to help you become the best-version-of-yourself. Every relationship, however formal or casual, long lasting or fleeting, is an opportunity for the people involved to further their essential purpose by becoming the-best-version-of-themselves.

What makes a good relationship? A good relationship is one where we are challenged and encouraged to become the-best-version-of-ourselves, while we encourage and challenge others to become all they are capable of being. What defines troubled relationships? Troubled relationships are those that lead us away from our essential purpose, those that encourage us to be lesser-versions-of-ourselves.

The full and dynamic experience of relationship is therefore dependent on a clear understanding of our essential purpose.

So, where do we start?

There is a question that you have probably already started grappling with, and whose answer may have set off some alarms for you. That question concerns your primary relationship. It may be with your husband or wife, your girlfriend or boyfriend, your partner, your significant other, your fiancée . . . but the question remains the same.

Is your primary relationship helping you to become the-best-version-of-yourself?

Are you helping the other person to become the-best-version-of-themselves, and are they helping you to become your best self?

Your first answer may very well be no. And that's okay; deeper examination will probably reveal that in some ways the relationship is indeed helping us become the-best-version-of-ourselves, but that in some other ways (that are perhaps more glaring) it is, quite simply, not helping us to do so.

The other very real possibility to consider is that as a couple you have never thought of your essential purpose. It may be that in a subconscious way you always knew that the primary purpose of your relationship was to help each other to grow, but together you have never articulated it. If that is the case, then this discovery of your essential purpose is the most important discovery of your relationship, and if you allow it to, it will mark the beginning of an extraordinary period in your relationship.

Whether you have been married for thirty-five years, have just become engaged, or have just started dating, place your essential purpose at the center of your relationship. Do so by placing it at the center of your decision-making process.

Life is choices. In every choice we choose the-best-version-of-ourselves or some second-rate version. With every choice, we can improve our relationship or diminish it. When faced with a choice, when an opportunity presents itself, whenever we have a decision to make, the first question we need to ask ourselves is, Which of the opportunities before me will help me become the-best-version-of-myself?

By constantly asking this question in the moments of the day, and then by living the answer, we place our essential purpose at the center of our lives and at the center of our relationships.

At the breakdown and breakup points of relationships, I often hear people say, "Nothing makes sense anymore." Why doesn't anything make sense anymore? Perhaps we need to ask, Did anything ever make sense?

Nothing makes sense anymore for these couples because they have lost sight of the essential purpose of their relationship. In many cases, they were never consciously aware of this great purpose. They may have enjoyed a mutual pleasure or some common interests, but their relationship never matured to include the great ambition of extraordinary relationships—the pursuit of our essential purpose.

Think on it for a few moments. Everyone knows that one in two marriages in the United States today ends in divorce or separation. This has sparked the cultural conversation regarding a "crisis in commitment." From here, the discussion has turned to the fact that during your career you are likely to change jobs six times more often than your grandfather did. The case is furthered by statistics that suggest people are waiting longer and longer to marry, and that, indeed, fewer people are marrying at all. People even seem unable to commit to and follow through on a simple diet and exercise routine. The talk of a crisis in our ability to commit gathers more and more momentum with every passing day. Yet the real crisis is not in the area of commitment, but in the arena of purpose. Without a clear understanding of our purpose, it is all but impossible to commit to anything and follow through on that commitment. It is purpose that inspires us to fulfill our commitments. We don't have a crisis in commitment; we have a crisis of purpose.

What keeps relationships together? A sense of common purpose keeps relationships together. When do relationships fall apart? When the sense of common purpose is lost.

In some relationships, the common purpose is simply pleasure, so that when the pleasure ceases, or a more appealing form of pleasure presents itself, the relationship ends. In other relationships, common interests provide the guise of a common purpose, but when our interests change the relationship often fades. A pattern that has intrigued me in recent years seems to be occurring more frequently; the breakup of couples after twenty-five, thirty, even thirty-five years of marriage. I have racked my brain and studied these relationships over time trying to understand them and found that the answer is surprisingly simple. These couples shared a common purpose in raising their children, and now that their children are raised, they find they no longer have anything in common. More importantly, they no longer have a common purpose. Their common purpose was a temporary one and has now evaporated, and as a result, so has their relationship.

The truth is that all relationships are based on a common purpose, whether that purpose is articulated or not. In some relationships, the common purpose is simply a matter of convenience; in others, it is money; in some, the common purpose is sex; in others, it is raising the children, but only in a very few relationships is it to help each other become the-best-version-of-ourselves.

Our primary relationship needs a common purpose, but not just any common purpose.

What is the difference between any of these common purposes and our essential purpose? The purposes we have just discussed are temporary, whereas our essential purpose never changes and never fades. We will always be striving to celebrate the-best-version-of-ourselves in every moment. It isn't a project that is ever finished. It is the striving that animates us—brings us to life.

If your primary relationship is based on a common purpose that is temporary, there is a pretty good chance that your primary relationship will be temporary, as well. But if you base your primary relationship on your essential purpose, which is unchanging and lasting, there is an equally good chance that your primary relationship will last. And not only survive, but thrive.

Place your essential purpose at the center of your relationships. If you get this right, a lot of other things just fall into place.

A relationship of any significance should be a dynamic collaboration. By striving to become the-best-version-of-ourselves, and helping others to do the same, we help to create a dynamic environment within the relationship that inspires us to reach for greater heights, encourages us and comforts us when we fall short, and celebrates with us when we succeed.

When we understand our essential purpose, a different set of values and priorities comes to the foreground. We become less preoccupied with questions such as: What's in it for me? What do I get out of it? We are able to focus more on questions such as: How can I help you become the-best-version-of-yourself? How can I love you completely and selflessly? How can I help you know and fulfill your dreams? How can I help you use your talents to the fullest? What are your needs, and how can I help you fulfill them?

If you really love someone you want nothing less than to see that person become all he or she is capable of being, and you are willing to do everything to help that person achieve his or her essential purpose.

Relationships, and marriage in particular, can be a very powerful forum for personal growth. But you and your partner have to agree to make it so. You have to want it, and you have to discipline yourselves to pursue it. If we do not consciously focus on improving our relationships, over time they can become tremendously detrimental to our personal growth. Like most things in this world, relationships can be the agents of tremendous good or incalculable destruction. The choice, as always, is ours.

Relationships should be governed by this one simple vision: the quest to help each other become the-best-version-of-ourselves. The more we allow the clarity of this simple vision to direct our lives and relationships, the more we will experience the passionate and purposeful lives we were created to live.

The great journey in relationships is from "yours and mine" to "ours." It is the great synthesis of two beings for one common purpose. The first step in this journey is establishing a mutually agreed-upon goal. Once that common goal has been agreed upon, a dynamic collaboration begins. The more noble and long-lasting the goal is, the more noble and long-lasting the relationship will be.

The most noble and long-lasting goal is to help each other become the-best-version-of-yourselves. This is the ultimate purpose and goal of relationship.

BETRAYAL OF SELF

The biggest problem in relationships is the betrayal of self. Every second person you meet wants you to compromise on who you really are. They want to buy it or trade for it, and they do so for personal pleasure or gain. So we must guard our true self above all else. But this will only be possible if we value our true self above all else.

Do you value your true self above pleasure? Do you value your true self above money and possessions? Do you value your true self above popularity and status?

What is more valuable than your true self? Nothing. Your true self is the custodian of your honor, integrity, and dignity. Without these things we are little more than pawns in other people's games and plans. If you don't have your self you have nothing. For if we betray our very self, how can we ever be true to anyone or anything?

When we behave in ways that are contrary to our values, beliefs, and principles, the result is inner conflict and shame. We then have to either resolve the inner conflict by living in accord with our values, beliefs, and principles in the future, or else flee from our shame. Flight from shame is of course impossible, because in a very real way it is an attempt to flee from ourselves. The story of many people's lives can be summarized into two parts: the betrayal of self and the flight from shame. For once we betray ourselves we run unceasingly from our shame, unless we can summon the humility to face our error and begin anew.

Guilt and shame serve to warn us when our behavior is inconsistent with what we hold to be good, true, and just.

Never did William Shakespeare pen truer words than the day he wrote: "To thine own self be true, / And it must follow, as the night the day, / Thou canst not then be false to any man."

Our first responsibility in relationship is, therefore, to be true to ourselves. From this flows our responsibility to help the people we love be true to themselves. The more authentic we are within ourselves, the more authentic we can be with those we love.

The problem is that it is so easy to lead someone to betray himself or herself. It may begin with something as simple as asking someone to lie. The lie may seem small, even insignificant—you may even convince yourself that it is necessary at the time—but with that tiny lie begins the betrayal of self and the eroding of character. For once the lie is told, we are obligated to live the lie. And once we have betrayed ourselves, if we are unwilling to humbly admit our mistake and correct our ways, we run from our shame.

A man's true self lies within his values, principles, morals, and ethics. He can't be his true self if you take him away from these things. If you do take him away from them, you can be certain of one thing: sooner or later, he will leave you to get back to his true self.

He will leave you to get back to his morals, ethics, principles, and values, because he can't live without them. Not happily. He will never have peace if he is separated from them, and the human spirit yearns for that peace. Our lives are a constant searching for that peace. It is the peace of being aligned with our true selves. It is the peace that all men seek, but that a rare few ever find.

Yes, we all like to experience the pleasures of this world. Certainly, one person enjoys pleasure as much as the next. But while we can live without pleasure, we can't live without our true self . . . and we can only find our true self in and through morals, values, principles, and the ethical way of life.

So if you move a man or a woman away from these things, sooner or later he or she will leave you. You may not even be the one who instigated his move away from his values and principles. The move may even be his idea. You may only be the witness to his betrayal of self. But none of us likes to share a room with the witness of our crimes. It makes us restless and uneasy, prevents the self-deception necessary to press on. All men and women flee from the witnesses of their wrongdoings.

Even if he does not leave you physically, he will leave you emotionally. He has to detach himself, to move away, to distance himself, for he is fleeing the scene of his own betrayal of self. If he does not leave you physically, you may end up wishing he had, for sometimes not leaving can be worse than leaving. Be certain that physically, emotionally, intellectually, and spiritually he will leave you a thousand times and in a thousand different ways, in order to get back to his or her true self. He can live without you, but he cannot live without his true self. Before too long, he will despise you, resent you, because you took him away from his true self, and now you represent a life that is contrary to his values and principles. He may find momentary pleasures in such a life, but the agony of being violently disconnected from his true self is unbearable.

If you really want to get someone to resent you, take that person away from her god—from her morals, ethics, values, and principles. Because sooner or later, whether she is aware of it or not at the time, she will want to get back to God and back to her true self. She may be prepared to abandon her true self and God briefly for pleasure, possessions, and popularity, but in the long run she is coming home. Nothing is more certain. It might take ten years for the person to realize what has happened, but sooner or later the crop you sow will be the crop you harvest.

Before you ask someone to compromise her principles and values, think long and hard.

It may seem that the person is willing to abandon his true self. He may do so willingly. You may think this is what he wanted. You may say to yourself that he agreed to it. It may even be true that the betrayal was his idea, and that he was its architect and engineer. But he will still resent you for it, even blame you, get rid of you because you remind him of his weakness, his failure, his shame. He will flee from you because in you he is reminded of the shameful moments when he abandoned his true self for the merely superficial realities of this life. It may very well not be your direct fault, but you become a reminder by association.

This is why it is so important to involve ourselves with people who have thought about life, people who have a sense of who they are and what they want, people who know what their values and principles are and know how to own them and live them in a real and personal way.

It may be that you are in a relationship where one or both of you have betrayed your true selves. Will she leave you? Will you leave him? Yes, without question, unless you can both come together, agree to help each other celebrate your true selves, and abandon the actions that previously led you to betray your true selves. What does it take? Humility. At the core of every solution to every problem, we will find a virtue. In this case, that virtue is the humility to admit how we have violated our values, principles, and morals (and perhaps the values, principles, and morals of the person we love).

Whenever possible, help those around you to celebrate their true selves. When you first meet people, try as hard as you can to understand what their values and principles are, and after honoring and defending your own true self, make it your first priority never to lead those people away from their true selves.

If you betray our very self, how can you ever be true to anyone or anything?

MAKING SENSE OF LIFE AND RELATIONSHIPS

Making sense of life and relationships in a world where we are constantly bombarded with conflicting information is difficult. That is why it is so important to carry with us an internal compass that allows us to assess the relevance of incoming data. What makes something relevant? It's relevant if it helps you become the-best-version-of-yourself.

From now on, before you put anything on your schedule, ask yourself: Is that going to help me become the-best-version-of-myself? You will be amazed at the clarity this one principle will bring to your life.

As you begin to center your life on your essential purpose, you will naturally and without thinking bring this clarity and direction to all of your relationships. Ask yourself each morning: How can I help my partner become the-best-version-of-himself/herself today? Each time you encounter someone during the day (whether it is a supermarket clerk, one of your children, a colleague at work, or a friend), ask yourself: How can I help this person to become the-best-version-of-himself/herself?

Your essential purpose is to become the-best-version-of-yourself. Place it at the center of your life. The meaning and purpose of a relationship is to help, challenge, encourage, and inspire each other to become the-best-version-of-yourselves. Place this at the center of your relationships.

Get this right, and you will be amazed by how everything else just falls into place.

CHAPTER THREE

⌑

YOU KNOW THE STORM
IS COMING

THE TREE ANALOGY

A tree with strong roots can weather any storm. In our relationships, the question is not, Is there going to be a storm? but, When is the next storm getting here? And when the next storm gets here, it's too late to sink the roots. When the storm hits, you've either got the roots or you don't.

Relationships are exactly the same. When a storm hits your relationship, you've either got the roots to weather the storm, or you don't.

Different people respond in different ways to the storms in their relationships. Some people run. We are all capable of this type of cowardice, and when someone acts in a cowardly fashion we are rarely able to change his or her mind. Others madly scramble about in an effort to sink roots. This is a natural and noble reaction. Still others pull up the roots that they have spent the years of their relationship sinking. This is madness, but crisis makes many temporarily insane.

What are the roots that will help our relationships weather the inevitable storms? Communication, appreciation, respect, a mutual willingness to serve, annual vacations are just a few. But there are too many to name; the list is endless. As with diets, there are hundreds of them, thousands of them. Which one works? Almost all of them will work for almost all people. Diets don't fail. People fail at diets. We get lazy and neglect the basic resolutions.

You may not know what the storm looks like, but you know the storm is coming. Now is the time to prepare.

Weathering the Storm

The roots that will help our relationships weather the inevitable storms include everything from taking walks together, date night, regular vacations, and praying together, to gratitude, respect, healthy confrontation, and discipline.

There's something powerful about exercising with your significant other. It may not be practical to do it every day, but should be possible once a week. It is powerful because in that simple activity you are both changing, growing, and exploring your untapped potential. The more activities you can do together that help you achieve your essential purpose, the more attuned you will be to the-best-versions-of-yourselves and the more you will be attuned to each other.

It is so easy to get carried away in the concerns of our daily lives and neglect each other. What's wrong with having a regular date night? Our lives are constantly gathering a momentum of their own; let's stop from time to time and make sure we are not rushing east at a thousand miles an hour looking for a sunset. The idea of a regular date night might seem regimented to those of us who like things to be a little more spontaneous, or perhaps that is just an excuse for our inability to commit to anything even as simple as dinner and a movie on a regular basis with the most significant person in our universe. The truth is, most relationships could use more one-on-one time. It's there for the taking, but we have to want it. We have to value time with our significant others above all the other things. We have to be willing to make sacrifices to make it happen. Life is choices. We have to choose that one-on-one time.

And I know how old-fashioned it may sound, but if we are really serious about experiencing intimacy with another person we need to share spiritual experiences; we need to pray together. Do you have any idea how few couples pray together? If you want to put your relationship in a whole different stratosphere, pray together. I'm not talking about going to church on a Sunday. You sit there and he sits there. You listen and pray. He listens and prays. You do it together, but not really. You haven't got the foggiest idea how God is challenging him to change and grow, and he hasn't the foggiest idea what is in your heart. But secretly you both like it this way, because this way you don't have to be accountable to anyone. You are, of course, accountable to God, but it's not like having someone living and breathing right beside you to help and challenge you to grow. So when I say we need to pray together, I mean we need to openly share our spirituality with each other. There may be great differences in the ways each person approaches this area of his or her life, but part of the great adventure of intimacy is learning about how we approach God and the things of the spirit.

JOY IS THE FRUIT OF APPRECIATION

You will never be happy until you learn to make gratitude part of your daily emotional and psychological diet. You will never have a great relationship until you learn to truly appreciate the wonder of another person. And you will never experience the depths of intimacy until you grow to be thankful for the opportunity to share the journey with another person.

My friend Hal Urban, a teacher in northern California high schools and the University of San Francisco for more than thirty-five years, tells a great story about making gratitude a habit.

"How many times a day do you complain?" he begins one of his classes by asking. There is some grunting and groaning, and then he asks his students to go the next twenty-four hours without complaining about anything. No complaints, valid or invalid. (The first reaction is usually a complaint about the assignment.) Each student is asked to carry pen and paper for twenty-four hours and record every time he or she complains, and about what.

The following day, Hal asks each student to guess how many people were able to keep from complaining. Each student writes a number down on a blank piece of paper, as does Hal. In a class of thirty students, their predictions run somewhere between six and twelve. Hal's prediction was always zero. For the first twenty-three years he used this exercise, he was always right. Today, through his seminars and presentations, Hal has challenged more than seventy thousand people of all ages to try the exercise and has found only four people who were able to go twenty-four hours without complaining.

But that isn't the end of the experiment.

Hal then asks two simple questions: What was the purpose of the assignment? and What did you learn from the exercise?

From class to class and group to group, the same answers almost always emerge. The first answer is usually "You wanted to show us how much we complain." And the second answer is usually "I learned that I don't really have much to complain about. What I complain about is stupid."

We all complain too much, and yes, our complaints are mostly insignificant, showing a monumental ingratitude for the incredible opportunities we have and the wonder of life. Whom do we complain to the most? The people we supposedly love the most. Whom do we complain about the most (either out loud or to ourselves)? The people we supposedly love the most.

Our complaints are poisoning our relationships. Try going twenty-four hours without complaining.

Hal's gratitude assignment has a second part. After the discussion, he hands out a piece of paper that reads, "I'm thankful for . . ." across the top. Below it are three columns. In the first, labeled "Things," the students are asked to list all the material things they are glad they have. In the second column, "People," they are asked to list all the people in their lives, past and present, whom they appreciate. The third column is simply labeled "Other," and in it the students are asked to list anything that doesn't fit into the first two columns.

The third column always perplexes them at first. The students ask Hal questions, and in turn he asks them questions. Before long the "Other" column is being filled with things like freedom, opportunities, friendship, intelligence, love, peace, health, family, talents and abilities, faith, God, beauty, kindness, and so on.

Part Three of the assignment is to read the list four times within the next twenty-four hours: after lunch, before dinner, before going to bed that night, and before going to school or work the next morning.

The next day, when the students arrive for class, they just look different. There are more smiles, bigger smiles; their eyes are open wider, and their body language is livelier. Hal says, "When we focus on what's right instead of what's wrong, life improves considerably."

What has got your attention?

What are you focused on in your relationships?

Over the next three days, try the assignment. Try not to complain for twenty-four hours. Take a blank piece of paper and make your "I'm thankful for . . ." list, but add another list to the back of that page. Make a list of all the things about your significant other that you are grateful for.

Next week, make a copy of the list and mail it to that person. Yes, mail it. Even if you live in the same house and sleep in the same bed.

Gratitude changes our lives. It changes the way we feel about ourselves, the way we feel about life, and the way we feel about others.

If we can summon the courage to speak our gratitude to others it will give them the encouragement they need to keep striving to become the-best-version-of-themselves. I have found that both children and adults beam when we catch them doing something right and praise them. There are 6 billion people on the planet and I suspect that 5.9 billion of them go to bed every night starving for one honest word of appreciation.

Learn to appreciate and praise those you love. We all need encouragement. Becoming the-best-version-of-ourselves can be a daunting task! Commit to complimenting your significant other for something you appreciate about him or her at least once a week. Make gratitude one of the roots that allow your relationship to grow strong.

I grew up in Australia and I was twenty-two years old before I experienced my first American Thanksgiving, with a large family in Medford Lakes, New Jersey. When it came time for each person around the table to say what he or she was grateful for, my eyes began to fill with tears. To hear each person express gratitude, from infant children who were just learning to speak, to grown men and women experiencing the pressures of daily life, was awe-inspiring.

Giving thanks warms the soul and reminds us that life is an extraordinary privilege. Joy doesn't come from having, but from appreciating what we have. You can possess all the treasures, pleasures, and blessings this world has to offer, but if you don't appreciate them they will never bring you any real satisfaction.

Joy is the fruit of appreciation.

RESPECT BUILDS TRUST

Beethoven. What comes to mind when you see or hear that name? What thoughts, ideas, and feelings does it conjure for you? When you think about who Beethoven was and what he accomplished, are you filled with a sense of awe? I think of his music and how it touched people in a very new and exciting way, and of its power to reach across the centuries and continue to touch and inspire people. Beethoven is synonymous with genius, excellence, brilliance, and the rare beauty of fine music.

Beethoven's home in Bonn, Germany, has been preserved as a memorial museum for more than a hundred years now. In one of the rooms is the very piano that Ludwig van Beethoven composed most of his greatest works upon. It is in a roped-off area carefully out of the reach of the thousands of eager visitors who pass through the museum every day. The piano alone is estimated to be valued at more than $50 million.

Years ago, a group of students was visiting from Vassar College. When one of the students came to the room that held the piano, she stopped and gazed at it with great desire, and couldn't resist the temptation to ask the guard to allow her to play it for just a moment. The guard allowed himself to be influenced by her generous tip, and let the young woman beyond the ropes.

Sitting down at the piano, she then proceeded to knock out several bars of the Moonlight Sonata. When she had finished, her classmates applauded, some sincerely and others in mockery, clowning around.

Stepping back through the ropes, the young woman turned to the guard and said, "I suppose over the years all the great pianists that have come here have played the piano?"

"No, miss," the guard replied. "In fact, just two years ago I was standing in this very place when Paderewski visited the museum. He was accompanied by the director of the museum and the international press, who had all come in the hope that he would play the piano.

"When he entered the room he stood over there, where your friends are standing, and gazed at the piano in silent contemplation for almost fifteen minutes. The director of the museum then invited him to play the piano, but with tears welling in his eyes Paderewski declined, saying that he was not worthy even to touch it."

That is reverence, a deep respect that causes us to stop and look beyond appearances and discover a greater hidden value.

When was the last time you gazed with reverence at the one you love?

Have you stopped recently to consider what your journey would be like without that person?

We brush by dozens of people on the street every day and we congregate tens of thousands at a time for sporting events; have we, perhaps, become immune to the absolute wonder of the human person?

The reflective heart and mind has reverence for people. But when we are caught up in the hustle and bustle of our busy lives, we become self-centered, obsessed with the urgent, and we lose that wonderful childlike ability to experience wonder, awe, and reverence. Something is lost when we misplace our ability to experience these things.

When we take time to reflect on the beauty of nature, the extraordinary wonder of the human being, and the great mystery that we possess the ability to both love and be loved, our natural response is reverence. From this reverence is born the respect that is an indispensable ingredient of all successful relationships.

To respect is to value people and things in their proper order. Respect is one of the great cornerstones of relationships. Respect fosters trust and encourages openness and honesty. We should show respect for other people even before they have done anything to deserve it, simply because they are human beings. Respect reminds people of their innate and extraordinary value even if they have forgotten it themselves. At the same time, we should always expect to have to earn the respect of others.

I have often heard people speak of their encounters with great leaders such as Mother Teresa and Gandhi, and almost to a person they say the same thing, "I felt that for those moments there was nothing else in the world but the two of us and our conversation. People were trying to pull at us, and there was a schedule to be keep, but she gazed into my eyes as if she didn't have a care in the world, as if nothing other than me existed."

Who doesn't like to be treated in that way?

How do such people do it?

The outer action of respect is born from the inner quality of reverence, and that reverence is the fruit of reflection, which helps us to see people and things in their true value. But you cannot make someone feel valued if secretly you think he or she is a nobody. We see this all the time in arrogant and self-serving leaders. We can spot them from a mile away, and our natural inclination is to distrust them.

Respect builds trust.

We nurture this respect in two ways.

First, simply learning to enjoy people. Taking the time to get to know them, listening more and speaking less, seeking to understand rather than to be understood. By accepting other people for who they are with all their quirks, understanding that they have had a different experience of life and that those different experiences have contributed to make them who they are today. With every encounter, seek to know people more: who they are, where they come from, what their story is, what their passions are, what are their hopes and dreams.

The second way we nurture respect is by taking time each day to sit in the classroom of silence, to reflect on the true value of people and things. Some people spend time in the classroom of silence by taking a long walk in a quiet place, others spend time in the quiet of their church; some have a big comfortable chair in a corner of their home that serves as their classroom of silence. But one thing is common to all of us: silence makes us take a look at who we are, where we are going, and the value we assign to relationships and things.

How often a child will disrespect a material possession because he or she doesn't know the value of the item, or how hard you had to work to earn the money to buy it. In this way, we are all still children. We are all ignorant of the real value of certain relationships and things in our lives. Sometimes we are simply oblivious to it; at other times, we simply become a little self-absorbed and forget or disregard the value of things, people, and opportunities. We all lose sight of the true value of things from time to time, and as we lose sight of the true value of things we lose respect—for ourselves, for others, for the many talents, possessions, and opportunities that we have in life, and for life itself.

IF THERE IS NO DISCIPLINE,
THERE IS NO LOVE

When you think of the word "discipline," what comes to mind? For many it is an overdemanding teacher or a controlling parent. Try to set that notion of discipline aside, and think of the discipline an athlete freely chooses to bring the best out of himself or herself. Nobody can give you discipline, or make you disciplined. Discipline is a gift we give ourselves.

Every aspect of the human person thrives on discipline, and relationships are no different. Discipline is the price life demands for happiness. Again, I am not speaking about pleasure, I am talking about lasting happiness in a changing world. You cannot be happy for any sustained period of time without discipline.

Discipline is the road that leads to fullness of life.

Consider the four aspects of the human person, physical, emotional, intellectual, and spiritual. When we eat well, exercise often, and sleep regularly, we feel more fully alive physically. When we love, when we give priority to the significant relationships of our lives, when we give of ourselves to help others in their journey, we feel more fully alive emotionally. When we read good books that expand our vision or ourselves and our vision of the world, we feel more fully alive intellectually. When we enter into the classroom of silence and come before God in prayer, openly and honestly, we experience life more fully spiritually.

Each of these life-giving endeavors requires discipline. To eat well requires discipline. To exercise regularly requires discipline. To think of other people's needs before our own wants requires discipline. We do not happen accidentally upon the activities that help us to become the-best-version-of-ourselves. We must choose them, and that choosing requires discipline.

Are you thriving? Or are you just surviving?

When are we most fully alive? When we embrace a life of discipline. The human person thrives on discipline.

Discipline awakens us from the hedonistic stupor of modern popular culture and refines every aspect of the human person. Discipline doesn't enslave or stifle us; rather, it sets us free to soar to unimagined heights. Discipline sharpens the human senses, allowing us to savor the subtler tastes of life's experiences. Whether those experiences are physical, emotional, intellectual, or spiritual, discipline elevates them to their ultimate expression. Discipline heightens every human experience and increases every human ability. The challenge of our essential purpose (to become the-best-version-of-ourselves) invites us to embrace this life-giving discipline.

Is discipline, then, to be considered the core of the human experience? No. The life of discipline is proposed not for its own sake, but, rather, as the key to making us free. Discipline is the key to freedom. It is easy to give in to the allure of the momentary pleasures that this world so readily offers, but all great men and woman know the value of delayed gratification. The heroes, leaders, legends, champions, and saints who fill the history books knew how to embrace discipline.

One of the great challenges of the art of living is to learn to discipline ourselves, but at this moment in history, gratification seems to be the master of most people's hearts, minds, bodies, and souls. We find ourselves enslaved and imprisoned by a thousand different whims, cravings, addictions, and attachments. We have subscribed to the adolescent notion that freedom is the ability to do whatever you want, wherever you want, whenever you want, without interference from any authority. Could the insanity of our modern philosophy be any more apparent?

Freedom is not the ability to do whatever you want. Freedom is the strength of character to do what is good, true, noble, and right. Freedom is the ability to choose and celebrate the-best-version-of-yourself in every moment. Freedom without discipline is impossible.

Is freedom, then, the core of the human experience we call life? No. Love is the essence of life. Love is life's great joy and her greatest lesson. Love is the one task worthy of life. We busy ourselves with so many things, while the one great task we set aside, ignore, neglect. Love is your task—to love yourself by striving to becoming the-best-version-of-yourself, to love others by encouraging them and assisting them in their quest to become the-best-versions-of-themselves, and to love God by becoming all you were created to be.

But in order to love, you must be free, for to love is to give your *self* to someone or something freely, completely, unconditionally, and without reservation. It is as if you could take the essence of your very self in your hands and give it to another person. Yet to give your self—to another person, to an endeavor, or to God—you must first possess your self. This possession of self is freedom. It is a prerequisite for love, and is attained only through discipline.

This is why so very few relationships thrive in our time. The very nature of love requires self-possession. Without self-mastery, self-control, self-dominion, we are incapable of love. We want to love, but without self-possession we are simply unable to do so. We are not free. We do not possess ourselves and so we cannot give ourselves. As a result, we preoccupy ourselves with all the externals of relationships and call those love.

The problem is that we don't want discipline. We want someone to tell us that we can be happy without discipline. But we can't. In fact, if you want to measure the level of happiness in your life, measure the level of discipline in your life. The two are directly related.

Think about it. Americans spent $30 billion last year on diet products. The only diet most of us need is a little bit of discipline. But we don't want discipline. We want someone to get on the television and tell us we can be happy and healthy without discipline, and we will pay any amount of money for it. We want someone to get on the television and tell us if we take this little pill twice a day we can eat whatever we want, whenever we want, and as much as we want, and still look like supermodels. It is another of the great myths of our modern popular culture, the idea that we can be happy without discipline. It's a lie, it's a myth, it's an illusion, and somewhere deep inside we know that.

Every step toward the-best-version-of-ourselves requires discipline.

We need a diet of the body, a disciplined way of eating that helps fuel the body and brings it toward maximum performance. But we also need a diet of the mind, a diet of the heart, and a diet of the soul. Only then are we ready for a serious relationship. With your self in hand, you can choose to freely and completely give yourself to another person in the mystery of love.

If you want to measure the effectiveness of your relationship, measure the discipline in it. If your relationship is filled with and driven by whims, cravings, fancies, and constant lusting after pleasure, you don't have love. These things don't help us become the-best-version-of-ourselves, and if we truly loved another person, we would never do or encourage anything that would prevent that person from becoming the-best-version-of-himself or herself.

To love, we must be free, and yet too often we are slaves. Love is a promise, but a slave is in no position to promise anything to anyone. Never believe a promise from a man or woman who has no discipline. They have broken a thousand promises to themselves, and they will break their promise for you.

Discipline is evidence of freedom, and freedom is a prerequisite of love.

Allow discipline to permeate every area of your relationship. Let discipline guide you as a couple in your approach to the foods you eat, the ways you exercise, the way you spend your recreation time, the amount of sleep you get, your finances, your sexuality, the way you raise your children, and the ways you explore and share your spirituality.

In the lives of successful people, we find that discipline is indispensable. Why would relationships be any different?

Is your primary relationship thriving or just surviving?

How much is discipline a part of that relationship?

Do you want a successful relationship?

What makes a successful relationship?

A successful relationship is built when two people are striving to become the-best-version-of-themselves, challenging and encouraging each other to become the-best-version-of-themselves, and inspiring others to pursue their essential purpose by the example of their lives and their love.

You are not just going to wake up one morning in a relationship like that. You have got to want it, and you had better want it bad. Your significant other has got to want it, and want it more than anything else. You have got to formulate a plan (which I will help you do in part three of this book) and you have got to work that plan every day with the discipline of a champion.

If there is no discipline, it's not love.

HOW MUCH SHOULD *WE* GIVE?

Many years ago I was dating a wonderful young woman, and on her college graduation day she gave me a copy of Shel Silverstein's book *The Giving Tree*. Katie was that type of person. On a day when everyone was giving her gifts, she was giving gifts to others. My parents and teachers had read the book to me dozens of times during my childhood, but at that particular moment the book struck a deep chord in me again.

At certain times in my life I have found myself to be too much like the tree—giving too much, in self-destructive measures; at other times I have found myself to be very much like the boy—absorbed in the moment, enjoying people, places, and things for who and what they are, giving and receiving joy; and still, at other times, I have found myself to be too much like the man that the boy becomes—taking with no regard for the needs of others.

The story powerfully raises one of the ever-present questions in relationships, How much should we give?

When a relationship is going well, the question may be in the back of our minds, but it seems unimportant and perhaps irrelevant. While the other person is giving freely and generously, we seem willing to give without restraint. But when the other person turns in on himself or herself and becomes self-interested, self-centered, and self-absorbed, we don't know if this is a passing phase or a new and permanent disposition and the question begins to loom in our hearts and minds. Once this turning in on self begins, a relationship can very quickly become transactional, and it easy for us to feel that we are being taken advantage of, even used.

In the best relationships we are able to talk about this inward turning and the negative impact it is having on the relationship. But we have all found ourselves, and will find ourselves yet again, in relationships where we are either unable to have this conversation or our plea falls on deaf ears. It is then that we begin to ask ourselves, Do I keep giving freely and without reserve? Should I draw back a little? These are important questions, but the real question is, What do we hope to achieve by our giving?

Giving is an intrinsic part of a relationship, it is an indispensable component of our personal happiness, and the joy of giving is one of the most emotionally intoxicating experiences of this life. The joy of giving is one of life's great virtuous pleasures. Yet we should never allow ourselves to lose sight of the reason for our giving. And, in fact, it is this reason that should set the bounds of our giving.

When a child comes to his father and asks for the latest video game, what will guide the father's decision? Will he ask himself, "Can I afford it?" or will he ask himself, "Will this game help my son become the-best-version-of-himself?"

Our giving should be governed by our desire to become the-best-version-of-ourselves and our desire to help others do the same. Our giving must therefore be restrained and directed, for disconnected from our essential purpose even something as good and noble as giving becomes useless, distorted, self-indulgent, even dangerous.

Should we give of ourselves in order to bring happiness to others? Absolutely.

Should we give to the point that our giving becomes self-destructive? No. I don't think we should. There will be times when we will be asked to give in ways that require us to forgo our own legitimate needs, just as a mother gives up precious sleep to feed her child. But this type of giving should be the exception and not the rule in relationships. And more than ever, when giving requires great personal sacrifice and the forgoing of our own legitimate needs, we must constantly be tempering our giving by asking ourselves, Is this going to help the other person become the-best-version-of-himself or herself?

How much should we give? It's a difficult question, and like all of life's difficult questions it should be answered with our goal and purpose in mind.

Sometimes we have to be willing to give completely and in ways that are self-diminishing, but not every day and not at the whim and abuse of other selfish people. Our giving should not be a blind and reckless kind. We should give with the other person's best self in mind.

Your relationships are like trees. You can cut them down for firewood and you will be warm today, but you can only do it once. Or you can nurture yourself and your relationships, and if you do, you will enjoy their fruits for many, many years to come . . . and every year the fruit will be sweeter.

Embrace the Mystery

A tree with strong roots can weather any storm. If you have not done so already, the day to start growing those roots is today. Gratitude, respect, and discipline are three powerful ways to ground and nurture your relationships. But keep in mind also, that trees sway in the wind. They are not rigid. Even the largest and strongest trees sway when the wind blows. Allow for uncertainty; you can be sure it will come. Find the lesson in the unexpected; it has come to help you in your quest to become the-best-version-of-yourself. Try to enjoy mystery; it will keep you young.

The present culture despises uncertainty, and so we waste endless amounts of time and energy trying to create the illusion of security and attempting to control the uncontrollable. We curse the unexpected because it interferes with our plans, even though it often carries with it the challenge we need at that moment to change and to grow into a-better-version-of-ourselves. In the same way, our culture has no time for mystery. If we cannot solve it or prove it, then we ignore it or discredit it.

"Life is not a problem to be solved, it is a mystery to be lived," wrote Kierkegaard. Your spouse is not a problem to be solved, your children are not problems to be solved, your boyfriend or girlfriend, your partner or fiancé is not a problem to be solved. They are mysteries to be accepted, encouraged, experienced, and enjoyed.

Relationships are not to be understood and fixed and solved; they, too, are mysteries to be enjoyed.

The best participants in the mystery we call relationship seem to be the people who don't need to understand everything, the ones who aren't out to prove anything, those humble enough to accept when they are wrong and hold their tongues when they are right, the people who don't have an agenda, who aren't in a hurry, and who don't need the credit when things go right and don't pass the blame when things go wrong.

These are the rare souls who seem to be able to hold their arms wide open and embrace fully the mystery of loving and the joy of being loved.

CHAPTER FOUR

༺☙

WHAT IS DRIVING
YOUR RELATIONSHIPS?

YOU AND YOUR RELATIONSHIPS

The happiest people on the planet are the men and women who have dynamic relationships.

This has been the one consistent discovery in my travels to more than fifty countries in the past ten years. No matter what continent you are on or what culture you are exploring, it stands as a self-evident and universal truth. The happiest people give focus and priority to their relationships, and as a result have a richer experience of relationship and of life.

Family is important to them; friendship is important to them. I have moved among the extremely well educated and the woefully uneducated. Educated people aren't happier than uneducated people. I have sat at meals with men and woman of extraordinary financial wealth and with those living in the cruelest poverty. The rich are not necessarily happier than the poor. I have lived among people who had seemingly little to worry about, people who had much to hope for in the future, and people under the death sentence of terminal illness and other tyrannies. The same truth is evident among all people, at all times, and in all situations: the happiest people are those who cherish the mystery of relationship.

John Wooden, the college basketball coach of note, once said in an interview with *Sports Illustrated:* "Why is it so hard for so many to realize that winners are usually the ones who work harder, work longer and, as a result, perform better?" It is true in sports, it is true in business, and yes, it is true in relationships.

There are winners and losers in relationships. I am not talking about the games that have become a seemingly intrinsic part of the modern dating scene. In a relationship, one person doesn't win while the other loses. It is absurd even to speak in such terms. Either both win, or both lose. That's why so much is at stake. That's why we feel so powerless and helpless at times in relationships. That's why it is so important to choose the right people to spend our limited time and energy in relationships with. When I speak of winners and losers in relationships, I speak of the reality that some couples win and other couples lose.

In terms of relationships we must then ask: why is it so hard for so many to realize that great relationships are usually the ones where people work harder, work longer, and as a result have better relationships? The reason is, perhaps, that we don't want to admit that the winning or the losing is a choice that is within our control. Perhaps we don't want to admit that the difference between a great relationship and a failing relationship is our choice . . . not individually, but as a couple.

The significance of positive relationships is not confined to the emotional realm, nor is it limited to the time we set aside for family and social activities. The power and influence of positive relationships spills over into every aspect of our lives.

People who are involved in a positive primary relationship are more effective and more efficient in the workplace; they are more involved in community activities, and they tend to be better parents, friends, siblings, children, colleagues, and citizens.

The opposite is also true. People who are involved in a primary relationship that is struggling are generally less focused in the other areas of their lives, and as a result they are less effective and efficient. More often than not, they are looking to have needs met that are not being met in their primary relationship. It is natural that they look to the workplace, or to their relationships with parents, friends, siblings, children, and colleagues in an attempt to have their need for intimacy met. But often the intimacy they are seeking is not appropriate to the relationship they try to extract it from. The result is, of course, further friction and frustration.

The state of our relationships has an impact on every aspect of our lives. You don't leave a struggling relationship at home when you go to work or school, and you don't check a tumultuous relationship at the door of your other friendships. If you have a relationship that is struggling, there's a good chance it is affecting many areas of your life. The troubled relationship may be with a spouse or significant other, or you may have a relationship with a colleague, friend, child, parent, or sibling that has fallen on rough times. Relationships affect us deeply, and a failing or struggling relationship can have a negative impact on the way we perform at work, the hope we hold for the future, the way we feel about ourselves, what we eat or don't eat, the way we spend our time, and every other aspect of our daily life. On the other hand, when we are thriving in our relationships, especially our primary relationship, we tend to carry a very positive atmosphere with us wherever we go.

A dynamic primary relationship doesn't just change the social aspect of our lives, it changes our whole lives by changing the way we see ourselves and the world.

This book is about giving you the tools necessary to create a dynamic primary relationship. The seven levels of intimacy provide a simple model—the strength of any good model is simplicity—but the process is not easy. Sometimes the biggest mistake we make is believing, at the outset, that the journey ahead is going to be easy. Such a traveler almost always comes unprepared and under-supplied.

You may be well into your journey and have discovered that you need to stop to get resupplied; you may be just beginning your journey; or you may be trying to decide whether you want to set out at all. Whatever may be the case, I am delighted that our paths have crossed and I hope that the ideas that fill the pages of this book will prove useful to you in your quest for intimacy.

It takes a lifetime to build great relationships and to learn how to sustain them. Along the way, there will be great moments of triumph and ecstasy and other moments of trial and heartache. This book is no quick fix and it doesn't contain all the answers. It is simply a tool to help you reconnect with your deep desire to be involved in great relationships.

Connecting with people in a powerful way is a skill that must be developed, nurtured, and practiced.

Most of what we do every day we do simply to survive. Relationships are what drive us to survive.

WHAT'S NOT WORKING IN YOUR LIFE?

W hat's not working in your life? It's one of the questions I start with during the opening sessions of my seminars and retreats. The reality is we all have areas of our lives that are not functioning the way we would like them to. And yet, our tendency is to ignore these areas, hoping they will go away or change. They won't. We need to face them, explore them, and wrestle with them.

The challenges that come our way in life are simply opportunities to change, to grow, and to become the-best-version-of-ourselves.

When I ask "What's not working in your life?" at my seminars, I always have people take a few moments to write down their answers. There is something powerful about writing these things down; it can very often be the first step toward solving or healing these areas of our lives. By simply writing them down, we start to own them and in some small way we begin to cast them out.

In the group setting, we then begin to discuss how different people answered the question. Invariably, every participant includes one or more relationships on their list. Later in the seminar, when I ask participants to rank the things that are not working in their lives, 90 percent rank a relationship in the number one position.

Relationships are either growing or dying. There is no middle ground. This is one of the governing principles of the universe. Everything is constantly changing.

Sometimes we may think that a certain relationship is just stagnating, but it isn't. It's dying, and if we don't do something to rejuvenate it that relationship will die. Over and over people say to me, "I feel my relationship with my spouse has been stagnant for ten years or more." A quick look at the way they speak to each other, the way they treat each other, the way they look at each other, and you discover their relationship died ten years ago. They just didn't acknowledge it.

So before we move forward, I would like you to set this book down for ten or fifteen minutes. Take out your journal, or your planner, or some blank writing paper, and make a list of all the relationships in your life that are important to you. Go through all the different areas of your life (home, family, work, school, church, and so on) and write a list of all the people who are important to your life.

Don't agonize over the person you forget to put on the list, because you are sure to forget someone. Make the list quickly. It doesn't have to be perfect or definitive.

Now, once you have made your list of the more significant people in the different areas of your life, I would like you to answer the question, Which relationships aren't working? Again, put together a list.

It is, of course, possible that you don't have a relationship that is seriously struggling at this time in your life. Take a moment to be grateful for that, but then turn your attention to those relationships you would like to improve in some way. Put together a list. Then, as we move through the rest of the book, keep your list handy.

The sensation we call love can expand or contract. It expands when it is nurtured and contracts when it is neglected. Dynamic relationships require effort and self-sacrifice and thoughtfulness, and if you and your partner are willing to bring these things to the table, your experience of love can expand endlessly and infinitely.

Infinite expansion is possible, but not in an infinite number of relationships. You have only so much time and energy, so you have to decide which relationships matter most. You have to be willing to opt out of certain relationships in order to give your most important ones the time and attention that they require and deserve.

It is also crucial to point out that the purpose of this book is not to keep your relationships together. Keep in mind that the purpose of relationships is not to sustain them at all costs; the purpose of relationships is to help people become the-best-version-of-themselves.

Some relationships are not worth saving.

This may seem harsh at first glance, but it is an elementary truth. Some relationships are simply not worth saving and some people come into our lives just to help us grow through a certain situation. So, just because you were once close friends doesn't mean you need to always be close friends. Just because you were best friends in high school or inseparable in college doesn't mean you are going to be (or even need to be) best friends forever. Some people come into our lives at a particular moment for a particular reason, and that is enough.

If a relationship isn't working, you have options. Life is choices. You can stay in the relationship and continue to let it die, you can abandon the relationship, or you can decide to transform the relationship into a dynamic collaboration.

YOUR PRIMARY RELATIONSHIP

Your primary relationship is generally the one you have with your significant other. Depending upon what stage you are in your life, this relationship could be with a boyfriend or girlfriend, a fiancé or fiancée, or a spouse. This primary relationship is your emotional home. It should be a place where you can go to relax and unwind, though you can be certain that from time to time work will need to be done around the house, and there are always certain emotional chores to attend to. But your emotional home (your primary relationship) should very much be a place where you feel comfortable to be yourself and to reveal yourself.

This primary relationship is our first source and opportunity for intimacy.

If you are single, then there is a very good chance that a number of secondary relationships are on a higher level for you than they are for people who are involved in a primary relationship. If, or when, you enter a primary relationship, it would be natural for you to become less involved in these secondary relationships. This is simply a matter of resource allocation. You have a limited amount of time to spend with family and friends, and a primary relationship at some point takes precedence over secondary relationships.

This is the dynamic that causes people to complain, "You never have time for us since you started dating so-and-so" or "She used to hang out with us all the time." These complaints tend to be exaggerated, but in any case, once we find ourselves in an important primary relationship we shouldn't feel guilty about spending less time with our friends and more time with our significant other. We don't completely ignore our friends because we are in a primary relationship, but it stands to reason that we will have less time to spend with them.

There are three questions you should ask about your significant other: Do you trust your partner? Do you believe that this person has your best interests at heart? Is this person helping you to become the-best-version-of-yourself?

If you trust your partner, why? What did he or she do to build this trust in you? Similarly, if you don't trust your significant other, it is important to try to pinpoint the reasons and to recall some specific situations that have led you to distrust him or her. Again, there is a certain power in writing these things down; it sometimes helps us to look at them a little more objectively. So if you have your journal or planner handy, take some time to answer these questions in writing.

If you noted that your significant other has your best interests at heart, what makes you believe that? On the other hand, if you don't believe your partner has your best interests at heart, what do you think is motivating him or her to be in the relationship with you?

And finally, if you believe that your partner is helping you to become the-best-version-of-yourself, in what ways is he or she doing that? Or, if you don't believe that your significant other is helping you become the-best-version-of-yourself, what are the things that he or she does that pull you away from your best self?

It is unlikely that you could both trust and not trust a person, but it is certainly possible that at some times your significant other has your best interests at heart and at other times he or she doesn't; similarly, it is certainly within the realm of probability that in some ways your significant other helps you to become the-best-version-of-yourself and in other ways he or she does not. It may be helpful to take time to write down your answers to these questions and reflect upon both the positive and negative aspects.

The next question really needs to be answered, first on your own, and then with your partner:

Is your relationship your top priority?

For some people, it isn't. For some people, work and career are the top priority. At some times in a person's life, depending on their chosen career, that may be necessary. Other people place their parents and siblings ahead of their primary relationship. This may be a valid approach at the beginning of a relationship, but at some point it would be unhealthy not to give priority to our primary relationship.

People put other things ahead of their primary relationship for all sorts of reasons, healthy and unhealthy. The important thing is that all those involved know where everyone stands. Sometimes the most fundamental assumptions are the cause of constant and ongoing friction in relationships. So, if your primary relationship is not your top priority, the next question is, Does your significant other know that?

Now that we know where our primary relationship ranks in our priorities, it is important to address the question of our significant other. Keeping in mind that you cannot simply ask this question in passing; you need to have a conversation. If you just ask the question in passing, chances are your partner will just say yes, because somewhere deep inside we all know that is the answer our partners want to hear. Rather than coming straight out and asking, Is our relationship your top priority? You might ask: What are the priorities in your life? This will help both of you to understand your relationship in relation to your other priorities.

Having discussed the general priorities in your lives, you can then move on to discuss the specific priority of your relationship. Within the context of your other priorities, you can then consider whether the way you live your day-to-day lives reflects the priority you claim to give to your relationship.

For example, if your husband says your relationship is his top priority, but he works eighty-five hours a week and is always tired and uninterested when he is home or with you, then the way he spends his days and weeks doesn't reflect that priority. Similarly, if you have been dating a woman for a long time and she claims that your relationship is top priority, but you see her only once a week and she is slow to return your calls, the reality is different.

In some of my seminars for business executives, I ask them to list the priorities in their lives. The most common priority order is: God, family, friends, work, other. We then make photocopies of one week from their day planners, give them five different color markers, and ask them to highlight the whole week according to how they spent their time. There is an enormous gap between what we claim are our priorities and how we spend our time.

Most parents would say that their children are a top priority, and yet recent studies show that on average parents spend less than sixteen minutes in conversation each week with their teenage children.

For most of us, there is an enormous gap between what we say is important and how we actually spend our lives. People who are living with passion and purpose have closed the gap between what they consider to be their priorities and how they spend their time. If you are going to have extraordinary relationships, then you have to decide to make them a priority by allocating significant time and energy to them.

Life is priority driven.

Whatever you place your attention on will increase in your life.

If you are constantly thinking and talking about everything you are grateful for in your life, the number of things you have to be grateful for will increase. If you are constantly preoccupied with all the things you don't have, the number of things you wish you had will increase. Human thought is creative. What we think becomes. Everything begins first as a thought in our minds.

If we are serious about giving priority to our relationship, we must first give it priority in our minds. Before all else, you must know what a great relationship looks like to you. You must begin by clearly identifying the qualities necessary to build and sustain extraordinary relationships.

That's what this book is about, building and sustaining extraordinary relationships. Anyone can have an ordinary relationship. Nobody wants an ordinary relationship, but that is what most people have.

Our primary relationship is the inner sanctum of our emotional lives. It is our first source of emotional support and our primary opportunity to develop and experience a deep level of intimacy. For most of us, our primary relationship will be the one chance we have in this lifetime to truly know a person, and in turn, to be deeply known by another human being.

We spend our days surrounded by trivialities and superficialities, constantly overloaded with information. With every passing day, to deeply know a person becomes more and more of a miracle.

BEFORE YOU BREAK UP

As I write, a fear keeps popping into my mind. In my some-times overactive imagination, I can see people coming up to me after one of my seminars and saying to me, "I read your book *The Seven Levels of Intimacy* and broke up with my boyfriend the very next day."

The reason I have this fear is because, as in all my writing, I am trying to illumine the ideal path. The truth, of course, is that few of us will attain this ideal path, but striving toward it ani-mates us. The word "animate" means "breathe life into." Ideals breathe life into us. They challenge us to reach beyond previously self-imposed boundaries and to become a-better-version-of-ourselves.

If your husband doesn't always have your best interests at heart, that doesn't mean that he doesn't love you, only that we can all be a little selfish from time to time. And if your girlfriend doesn't always help you achieve your essential purpose, it doesn't necessarily mean that she is not the one for you. It just means she doesn't understand that the more she helps you become your best self, the more you will be able to love her.

As you read this book, you may sometimes feel that I am en-couraging you to break from your primary relationship, and some-times that I am saying that staying with your partner is the only way. Both are legitimate reactions; we tend to process new infor-mation through the lens of our own experiences, past and present. But the purpose of this book is not to sway you one way or the other, it is simply to help and encourage you in the journey that is your life.

The first truth of relationships is that they all have problems. Your partner is not perfect and neither are you. Your children will never be perfect children and you will never be a perfect parent. If you cannot accept this elementary truth, you will spend your whole life chasing a figment of your imagination.

I see it all the time in certain friends, whom I call serial daters. One of them will start dating someone; everything is wonderful, until one day he actually gets to know the person a little, and perhaps she expresses an opinion that is a little "out there" (meaning that it is different from his). Before you know it, he has broken up with her. You want to shake him and say, "No, she wasn't perfect. But guess what? Neither are you."

All relationships have problems, so don't react by breaking off your relationship because of something you read in a book, mine or anyone else's.

If you're not happy, there is no point in just jumping into the next relationship. You have to try to work out why this one isn't working, or why the last one didn't work. You also have to give some serious thought to why you ended up in this relationship that isn't working. You are not completely responsible, but neither is your partner. It also may help to look at other past relationships. Is a pattern emerging? Why do you end up in relationships like this?

It may very well be that what you need to do is end your relationship, and if this book is what brought you to that realization and it is the right thing for you to do—wonderful! But make sure you are doing it for all the right reasons, not just chasing another illusion.

SECONDARY RELATIONSHIPS

B eyond our primary relationship we are all involved in literally hundreds of secondary relationships. Some are very important to us, like the relationship between parents and children; others may be relatively insignificant, like your relationship with the security guard where you work. That the relationship is not significant doesn't mean you are not friendly and courteous; it simply means the relationship doesn't have a high priority.

Higher-level secondary relationships could include those with parents, children, siblings, in-laws, friends, colleagues at work, your employer or employees, or perhaps a business partner.

Our primary relationship tends to have a tremendous impact on our secondary relationships, and vice versa. If your husband has just told you he wants a divorce, you can be sure this is going to affect the way you relate to just about everyone else in your life. If your girlfriend has just been told she has a brain tumor, that situation is a part of your relationship, and it will affect the way you go about your daily activities and relate with others. If your wedding is six weeks away and you're not sure you can trust your fiancé, that's going to affect the way you relate to people.

These things affect our relationships with others by influencing what we talk about with them, how we filter and process what they say to us; and they significantly affect the level of energy we have to help others deal with their emotional struggles.

Many years ago, I was dating a young woman while at the time I had a particularly bothersome employee. The employee was unreliable, untrustworthy, and didn't take instruction well, but overnight reallocation of her role and responsibilities was not possible. I didn't realize how frustrated I was, nor did I realize how much it was affecting the other areas of my life. I certainly didn't realize how much I had been discussing it with my girlfriend. One night we were out to dinner and as I was talking about my employee, a look came across my girlfriend's face. "You know we spend more time talking about her than we spend talking about us!" she said. So the negative relationship with my employee was damaging my relationship with my girlfriend.

Primary and secondary relationships have a way of influencing each other. Pleasant and unpleasant things happen to us every single day of our lives. Great relationships magnify the good things that happen to us and make the unpleasant things bearable.

When something wonderful happens to you, who are the first people you want to tell?

When tragedy strikes, which people do you want to be with?

Whom do you want at your bedside keeping you company when you are sick?

Who encourages you when you fail?

Who challenges you gently to succeed?

Whose life do you want to significantly impact with your life?

Life is a limited experience, and yet, there is an unlimited number of people, places, and things to experience in your limited time.

In the arena of relationships, we also have a limited amount of time and unlimited opportunities. There are almost six billion people on the planet; you cannot have a personal relationship with each of them. You must choose.

Each day I receive hundreds of e-mails. I could sit at my computer all day for the rest of my life replying to e-mail, or I can write this book. I choose the book. The reason is that I believe the book is a more significant contribution than the thousands of e-mails I could send in the time it takes to write. I choose to write the book because it is a deeper communication, and in a mysterious way it is a chance for you and me, reader and author, to be intimate with each other even though we may never have met.

Every day we make choices, and in those choices we assign priority ranking to the different activities and relationships in our lives. We can try to do everything, and perhaps we can even end up doing many things, but we will excel at nothing. The colloquial label for this human tragedy is "jack of all trades, master of none." We see this all the time with children who want to be involved with every activity. They play soccer and baseball, take piano and karate lessons, participate in the school play, write articles for the school paper, and take art lessons. They do many things, but they never learn the discipline of any one thing. They float along with talent instead of refining that talent with discipline. They do many things, but excel at nothing. To a certain extent such experimentation is a part of childhood, but only to a certain extent. At some point, we should all bring an order to our lives that allows us to celebrate what makes us unique. Alternatively, we can bring our focus to one great task, to one passion, to one pursuit, and if we have chosen our one pursuit with an understanding of our talents and abilities and pursue it with discipline we will only do one thing, but we will excel at that one thing. The pursuit of excellence breeds character. The pursuit of variety does not.

Sometimes one is better than many.

The same is true in relationships. We can be friends with everyone and spread ourselves around very thin, but we will have no great relationship and no extraordinary experience of intimacy. Or we can bring focus and priority to a handful of relationships and explore the wonders of love and intimacy in the context of those relationships.

Sometimes less truly is more.

The significance of positive relationships in our quest for happiness cannot be understated. Positive relationships make every trial bearable and every triumph sweeter. Positive relationships influence every aspect of our lives and are the trademark of all happy lives.

WHO ENERGIZES YOU?

One of the great myths of the twentieth century was that time is our most valuable resource. The propagation of this myth led us to read books, listen to tapes, and attend courses about time management. We all invested in planners to help organize our time, and later we reinvested in Palm Pilots. We were told, "Time is money." "Don't waste time. Life is time." "Guard your time." "Plan your time." "Defend your time." "Wasting time is wasting life."

Most of this is true to some extent, but time is not our most valuable resource. The equality that is so often spoken about by politicians but rarely found in our modern world actually exists with respect to time. You get twenty-four hours a day and I get twenty-four hours a day. Nobody gets more. It doesn't matter how much money you have; you still get only twenty-four hours. It doesn't matter how well you kick a football or who your parents are; you still get just twenty-four hours. Equality. But some people do an awful lot more with their twenty-four hours than others do. Why? Energy is our most valuable resource, not time.

Energy is one of the most important factors for us to consider in relationships. What types of people energize you?

I'm energized by people who are smarter than I am, people who know things I don't know, people who have experienced things I haven't, people who have met men and women of great achievement and extraordinary character and can tell me a little about them. People who have great relationships energize me. People who have achieved extraordinary things energize me. People who know exactly what they want energize me. I am energized by people who are at peace with themselves and their God, people who have learned to live with their inner demons and at the same time shine. People struggling against the odds energize me. People who are willing to give everything to pursue a dream energize me. Silent heroes energize me. I am energized by people who go out of their way to commit random acts of kindness. People who are striving to become the-best-version-of-themselves energize me.

Who energizes you?

Why do they energize you?

It's important to know what types of people energize you and what types of people drain your energy. It's also important to know why different people affect your energy level in different ways.

It is also important not to confuse people with their environments. Some environments energize us at first, but only temporarily. The unknown worlds of rich and famous people can energize those of us who are not used to them, but that energy is an illusion that doesn't last. Similarly, if you are dating someone who takes you to all the best restaurants, buys you wonderful gifts, and takes you on trips to exotic places, you have to be careful not to fall in love with the lifestyle. You have to be sure that it is the person that interests you, not the lifestyle.

Life is the constant using and replenishing of energy. Physically, emotionally, intellectually, and spiritually, we are constantly using and replenishing energy.

Relationships can be tremendously energizing, but they can also be very draining. Too often it is the lower-level secondary relationships (the doorman, the bank teller, our customers, the telemarketer) that drain our energy and leave us spent. As a result, our primary relationship (spouse, girlfriend/boyfriend, significant other) and higher-level secondary relationships (children, parents, siblings) tend to suffer.

We may feel that our primary relationship drains us. We may believe that our higher-level secondary relationships drain us. The truth is, however, that we are probably drained before we get to our primary relationship and our higher-level secondary relationships. For example, a man comes home from a long day at the office and his wife wants to tell him about her day and his children want him to play catch or help with their homework. He feels pulled in many directions and concludes that his primary relationship (with his wife) and his higher-level secondary relationships (with his children) are draining him. The reality is that his energy was already drained when he got home.

In our reactionary world, it is then a natural progression for us to say that the man had to go to work—to pay the bills, to support his family—and that is why his energy is drained, and that is simply the way of the world. But if we are brutally honest with ourselves, we come to realize that we allow people and situations to upset our equilibrium and rob us of our energy. Life is choices. Everything is a choice. We cannot choose the way other people speak and act, but we can choose how we respond to the ways other people speak and act. We can respond calmly or angrily. And how we choose to respond to people controls the energy valve. Get angry, flip the valve, and you can almost instantly feel the energy rushing out of you like the air from a balloon. Stay calm and you can feel an inner strength growing, and an energy being created and consolidated.

What people do and say doesn't generally affect our energy level nearly as much as how we respond to what they do and say. We cannot control what other people do and say, but we can control how we respond. And by controlling how we respond, we control the energy.

Energy is an important part of intimacy. On a foundational level, intimacy is an exchange of energy. Knowing what energizes us and what energizes the people we love is one very powerful part of building and sustaining a dynamic relationship.

To be in tune with who and what energize us is an important step in the process of self-knowledge. It requires an awareness that is formed through self-observation. Most people, consumed with themselves, are completely oblivious to how the things they do and say affect the people around them, for better or for worse.

What sorts of people energize you?

How do the people in your immediate circle energize you?

How do those same people drain your energy?

Over the next few days, take note of which people and situations energize you and which ones drain your energy. Also, try to be aware of whether you are energized or drained by the person, the situation, or the way you yourself are responding to them. Learning what types of people and situations energize you, and what types of people and situations zap you of your energy, can powerfully transform the way you relate to people.

Energy is our most valuable resource. The more energy we have, the richer and more abundant our experience of life becomes. Energy is important to the success of your relationships. It's hard to be a good person when you are stressed out and tired. "Fatigue makes cowards of us all," Vince Lombardi observed. It is hard to be kind, thoughtful, gentle, and compassionate when you are tired. Finding ways to constantly replenish our energy is critically important to our relationships.

Intimacy should energize you. Not all the time, of course. Sometimes relationships can be more draining than anything else in this life, but as a general rule, intimacy should energize us. One sign that we have reached great heights in our quest for intimacy is that we know how to energize each other. Knowing how and when to energize each other is a sign of seventh-level intimacy.

CHOOSING FRIENDS AND PARTNERS

If you had to do it all over again and begin a primary relationship right now, how would you do it differently? Yes, it's a wildly hypothetical proposition for many of you, but it's not a bad place to start. It is one way to ascertain what you think is missing from your primary relationship, and what you really want from a relationship. If you take the question seriously, you will find it tells you a lot about your primary relationship and about who you are and what is important to you as an individual. It will also very likely tell you something about how your priorities have changed over time.

If you are single, then this is a very practical exercise. The great multitudes of people passing through this world don't know what they want. Most people know what they *don't* want, either because they have it now or because they have had it in the past. It is painful and impossible to eliminate all the undesirable possibilities through experience. Knowing what you do want can save you a lot of heartache.

Every choice becomes significantly easier once we commit to placing our essential purpose at the center of our lives. When we choose a partner for life and friends to make the journey with, we should do it with our essential purpose clearly in mind.

There are only two genuine unspoiled motives for friendship. The first is that you can help the other person become the-best-version-of-himself or herself. The second is that the other person can help you achieve the same. In an ideal friendship, both exist. What is preferable in friendship is necessary between partners. You cannot form a primary relationship simply because you can help the other person. Marriage, the most common form of primary relationship, is two people challenging and encouraging each other to become the-best-version-of-themselves, and then in turn raising children and educating them to become the-best-version-of-themselves.

Will this person help me become the-best-version-of-myself?

Am I in a unique position to help this person become the-best-version-of-herself (or himself)?

Don't you wish your children would use these criteria to choose their friends? Don't you wish your children asked themselves, "Will this person help me become the-best-version-of-myself?" before they admitted people into their inner circle?

Do you use these criteria?

Or do you choose your friends for any number of shallow and superficial reasons?

Everything from popularity to opportunity motivates friendship. What are your motives? Who are your friends, and why are they your friends? What are your friends' motives for having you as their friend?

This is why I spend so much of my time and energy in high schools, teaching young people to base their decisions on guiding principles and lasting values, rather than on fleeting whims, cravings, and fantasies. Many of the most important decisions we make concern who we spend our days, weeks, months, and years surrounded by. Sooner or later we all rise or fall to the level of our friendships.

Let me tell you about some of my friends. Throughout my life I have been extraordinarily blessed with the people whose paths have crossed with mine. Today I have friends all over the world who encourage, challenge, and inspire me to become the-best-version-of-myself.

At the top of that list at this time in my life is a couple who live in northeastern Pennsylvania. I met Janie and Tony several years ago. Janie's great contribution has been to transform the way I eat, with her book *Essential Eating*. When we first met I ate very, very poorly. But over time Janie continued to challenge me to see food as fuel and to take better care of the body that has been entrusted to me.

Tony is a recovering alcoholic. He hasn't had a drink in twenty years, but his understanding of the addictive mind is inspired and absolutely fascinates me. Tony has been to hell and back through his addiction and now makes himself available to others as they struggle to overcome the tyranny of addiction. The thing about Tony is that he will never tell you what he thinks you should do. He will just ask you questions, and let you talk it through, until you arrive at the course of action that will help you become the-best-version-of-yourself. It is a way of relating to people that takes tremendous patience, and in this crazy busy world I find it awe-inspiring.

What attracts me to both Janie and Tony's friendship is the way they are able to honor and enjoy me as an individual without ignoring the public aspect of my life. Some people just want me to be the "Matthew Kelly" they have discovered in books and through my talks and seminars, while other people just want me to be the "Matthew" whom they grew up with or went to college with. Those who want me to be Matthew Kelly tend to ignore the normal person behind the name, and those who just want me to be Matthew tend to ignore the public aspect of my life. But I need friends who don't ignore or negate either part of my life, friends who can share both the ordinary personal moments and the rather extraordinary public moments with me. Tony and Janie are two such friends.

Another great friend of mine is Dan. I could tell Dan anything and I honestly believe he wouldn't judge me. It is quite extraordinary. When I was first getting to know him, it was my natural condition to distrust such overwhelming and complete acceptance, but over time experience has consistently affirmed that Dan is the least judgmental person I know. I want to have that quality. I want to be as nonjudgmental and accepting of the people in my life as he is; I want to make people feel the way he makes me feel, completely accepted. So I love being around Dan. He energizes me and silently inspires me to change and grow.

Let me tell you, maintaining a nonjudgmental attitude is harder work than you might think.

My friend Nick is more genuinely interested in other people's lives than anyone else I know. When Nick asks you, "How are you?" or "How was your day?" it is not a conversational platitude; he is genuinely interested and wants to know. Nick's fiancée teaches Tae-bo, so on Tuesday nights you can find Nick and me sweating it out at the back of her class and catching up on the happenings of our lives.

I'm no slouch on the tennis court, but my friend Ken can make me work for it every time we play, and he is almost twice my age. He is a great athlete and has a competitive spirit, and I love that. I love being around people who can stretch me beyond my comfort zone in any area of life. Ken is one of them and I am always energized when we spend time together.

Mark is a relatively young man of extraordinary accomplishment in the world of business; he is constantly assisting me in two ways that I greatly value. First, he challenges me to spend my time on the things that matter most, to focus on my areas of genius and employ capable people to do whatever isn't within those areas.

Second, Mark also has a rare understanding of my work and is constantly encouraging me to refine the vision for the foundation. Mark is constantly asking, "What will The Matthew Kelly Foundation be doing a hundred years from now?" His is a powerful friendship.

Friendship is powerful when we approach it trying to help each other become the-best-version-of-ourselves. In one way or another, all of my friends are better people than I. That's what makes them great friends. The sheer gravity of their character draws me toward the-best-version-of-myself. Sooner or later, we rise or fall to the level of our friendships. Surround yourself with people who are better than you in a hundred different ways and allow the force of their character to inspire you to change, grow, and strive to become the-best-version-of-yourself.

How should we choose our friends? Upon what criteria should

we choose a partner? Choose with the best-version-of-yourself in mind. Place your essential purpose at the center of your life and make every decision with your essential purpose in mind.

IT'S NOT TOO LATE!

In the first part of this book we have covered a lot of relationship territory. We have also asked many soul-searching questions. I hope that the questions I have raised have caused you to put the book down and think from time to time. In the days and weeks ahead, I hope those questions continue to prod at you. Questions are an important part of the human experience.

Sometimes you read things that are so clear, and so real, and so true, that they change you even as you read them. Every writer dreams of writing in such a way. If you have ever read something that touched you so powerfully and moved you so instantly, you can remember the very place you were sitting when you read it. I have had many experiences like this; if you were to look along the shelves that hold the books that have touched me most deeply, I could tell you where I bought them and where I was when I first read them.

I was on an evening flight out of Los Angeles, bound for Sydney, when James Allen's *As a Man Thinketh* first made me sit up straight and think. Hemingway first captured me in this way with *A Moveable Feast* during a weekend getaway in Palm Beach. Sometimes a whole book can have this effect on you; at other times, you may be struck by a phrase or a paragraph. I was in my final year of high school when I first read the whispered cry Joseph Conrad put in the mouth of Mr. Kurtz just before he died as he looked back on his life in *Heart of Darkness:* "The horror! The horror!"

But I bring all this up now because of something I read last year. The week before, I was having lunch with my agent and we were talking about books that had profoundly impacted our lives. In the course of the conversation he had mentioned Hugh Prather's *Notes to Myself.* I hadn't read it—I had never heard of Hugh Prather—and I was curious, so I ordered a copy online later that day.

When the book arrived, I sat in the large leather chair in my study where I write. As I turned back the cover of the small paperback and flipped through the pages to assess the landscape ahead, I remember thinking, "This is my kind of book." I don't know why I thought that; perhaps it was the way the thoughts were generously placed on the pages. But that is the sort of thing you remember when you read something that changes you even as you read it.

I only read one page of Prather that day, the first page. Fifty-five words, actually. I read it. Then I read it again. Then I sat there for a very long time and just thought about it. I don't know why it struck me the way it did, but I find it is particularly relevant to our conversation now.

> *"If I had only . . .*
> *forgotten future greatness*
> *and looked at the green things and the buildings*
> *and reached out to those around me*
> *and smelled the air*
> *and ignored the forms and the self-styled obligations*
> *and heard the rain on the roof*
> *and put my arms around my wife*
> *. . . and it's not too late."*

The contrast is powerful between the ways we complicate life with our "self-styled obligations" and the simple pleasures like listening to "rain on the roof" and putting our arms around the one we love. But it is at the moment when regret unexpectedly collides with a new chance and hope for the future that I am changed each time I read this piece. It changes me as I read it. It reminds me of what is most important and realigns my priorities.

It's not too late, and that is wonderful. Whatever problems your relationships contain, it is not too late. Simply remember this: if you're not part of the solution, you're part of the problem.

It's not too late. Not too late to be together, not too late to be apart. Not too late to go boldly out into the world and pursue the-best-version-of-yourself!

Every moment is just another chance to turn it all around. It's not too late, and that is a truly wonderful thing.

CHAPTER FIVE

⌘

THE OPPOSITE OF
LOVE IS NOT HATE

WHAT IS DESTROYING
MODERN RELATIONSHIPS?

The opposite of love is not hatred. The opposite of love is indifference. Hatred is an extreme that destroys only a handful of relationships, but indifference destroys millions. Hatred isn't responsible for the slow poisoning of relationships that we see and experience all around us in the world today. Indifference is poisoning our relationships. Indifference is driving a wedge between husband and wife, parent and child, friend and neighbor, employee and employer.

"Whatever!" Think about this simple expression, which has become one of the most common colloquialisms of our age. "Whatever!" has become the creed of a whole generation. What does it mean? It means "I don't care." It means "Leave me alone." It means "I can't be bothered." It means "I am indifferent."

Indifference is the most destructive force at work in our modern lives and relationships.

Where there is indifference, there is no passion. Indifference destroys all energy and enthusiasm for the great pursuits of life. Where there is indifference, there is no sense of purpose. Nonpurpose is the purpose of indifference. When we become indifferent to the passions and purpose of our lives, we begin to lead what Thoreau described as lives of quiet desperation. When couples and partners become indifferent to each other, indifferent to the passions and purpose of their relationship, their relationship very quickly becomes a place of misery.

The opposite of indifference is love. Indifference separates; love unites. Indifference doesn't care; love cares deeply. Indifference is hopeless; love is full of hope. Indifference is cynical; love believes. Indifference despairs; love rejoices. Indifference cannot be bothered; love gets involved. Indifference is scarcity; love is abundance. Indifference is tired; love is energetic.

Hatred is not the great enemy of our relationships; it is indifference we must all reckon with if we are going to pursue and have dynamic relationships. When you meet this indifference in a person whom you care about deeply, it is like trying to walk through emotional quicksand. You don't know what indifference is until you have deeply loved a person who is indifferent to you and your relationship.

What is the cure for indifference? Love. But let me warn you now, lest you form an illusion that will later be your undoing, that to love a person out of indifference requires the patience of Job.

Indifference represents soulless living. Love is the fruit of soulful living.

We must turn our attention to soulful living in every area of our lives, not just in the area of relationships. Soulful living sets us free from the great indifference that has beset so many good men and women of our age. Soulful living liberates us from desperation.

Our culture tries desperately to convince us, with the full force of advertising and the media, of the myth that fun, excitement, pleasure, and the constant purchasing of possessions will free us from this desperation. But in truth, these things only mask the problem, making us feel the desperation ever more deeply.

Soulful living liberates us from the disease of indifference. Soulful living sets us free from the chains of quiet desperation. We must therefore ask ourselves, What does it mean to live soulfully? What does it mean to have soulful relationships?

Everything we do every day can be done soulfully, if we approach it with our essential purpose in mind. Most of us spend our whole lives working, and most people are miserable in their work. Why? Some would have you believe that it is because their work is not exciting enough, others would say it is because they don't earn enough money, and others yet would try to convince you it is because their work is meaningless. The reality is that they fail to connect their work with their essential purpose.

Everything has value only inasmuch as it helps you and me become the-best-version-of-ourselves. Granted, some work is, in and of itself, more meaningful than other work. Feeding the starving people of Africa or developing a cure for cancer would seem objectively more meaningful to most people than cleaning the streets. But any honest work can become infinitely meaningful when we connect it with our essential purpose. Even the most meaningless work, if honest, can be infused with the meaning of our essential purpose.

If a man sweeps the streets for his entire life, but every day he works hard, works well, and pays attention to the details of his work, he will become a-better-version-of-himself through that work. Another man, who serves as president of a large corporation, earning enormous amounts of money, but at the same time is consumed by greed and laziness, will become a-lesser-version-of-himself with every passing day. Which man has more meaningful work? The street cleaner's work is infinitely more meaningful than the executive's. The value of every activity should be measured by how it affects our essential purpose. In this example, there is no question that the street cleaner is living more soulfully than the businessman.

Exercise is soulful. Eating foods that fuel and energize the body is soulful. When we take care of ourselves physically, we live soulfully. Emotional vitality is a sign of soulfulness. Reading great books is soulful. Soulful people have intellectual curiosity. Tending to our souls, exploring the life of the spirit, is soulful living.

Soulful living animates the human person—it brings us to life—and soulful living is achieved by connecting the seemingly trivial activities of our everyday lives with our essential purpose. Washing the car is just washing the car, until you decide to do it to the best of your ability because doing so will help you become the-best-version-of-yourself. Cooking dinner for your family is just cooking dinner for your family, until you decide to do it to the best of your ability and to make a meal that will help you all become the-best-version-of-yourselves.

Even the most trivial activities of our lives take on great meaning when we approach them with our essential purpose in mind.

We need to bring this soulfulness to our relationships. Even the smallest acts should be done with an absolute commitment to the essential purpose of relationships. What does it mean to love a person? To love a person means to do everything within your power to help that person become the-best-version-of-herself, and never to do anything that would hinder her from achieving this great essential purpose. There is no room for indifference in a soulful relationship. Living soulfully means doing everything with your essential purpose in mind. Soulful relationships revolve around helping each other become the-best-version-of-yourselves. And soulful relationships require soulful people. You cannot be soulful in your primary relationship if you are not soulful with your children. You cannot be soulful with your lover if you do not approach your work soulfully. You cannot turn soulful living on and off. Soulfulness is a way of life, which once tasted becomes an obsession.

Soulful people have large and generous hearts, and they lavish their love without discrimination upon the people who wander into their lives. They live in a world of appreciation and abundance, they energize those who cross their path, and their love of life is contagious.

Are you living soulfully?

LOVE ISN'T A FEELING . . . IT'S A CHOICE

While I was writing this book, a young man approached me after one of my seminars to seek my counsel. He was twenty-seven years old; he worked hard, loved his wife and was faithful to her, and had three wonderful children whom he loved very much. Two weeks earlier, his wife had told him that she wanted a divorce. When he asked her why, she told him that she didn't love him anymore. He asked her whether there was someone else, and she said there wasn't. Then he asked her whether it was something he had done, and she told him that it wasn't his fault, that he was a good father and a good husband, but that she just didn't love him anymore. It's a sad situation, and a common one.

Love is not a feeling. From when we are very young, through powerful mediums such as movies and music, we are conditioned to believe that it is. The result of this conditioning is that we allow our actions to be dictated by our feelings. Rather than asking ourselves whether a particular person is going to help us become our best self, we simply allow our feelings to take us wherever they will

at any particular moment. And I don't know whether you've noticed it, but feelings are one of the most inconsistent aspects of the
human person.

Our feelings shouldn't direct our actions and our lives. Our
actions should be driven by our hopes, values, and aspirations;
above all, they should be driven by our essential purpose. People
who are driven by feelings are dangerous. They are undisciplined, inconsistent, and unreliable. But people who are driven
by their values and a clear understanding of their essential purpose are to be treasured. They are disciplined, consistent, and re-
liable.

So if you want to be surrounded by people who are inconsistent and unreliable, choose your friends, your colleagues, your employees, and your significant other on the basis of feelings. But if
you want to be surrounded by people who are consistent and reli-
able, choose friends, colleagues, employees, and a significant other
who live value-driven lives—they will help you become the-best-
version-of-yourself.

Love is a choice, not a feeling. Feelings come and go, and if we
choose to base our most important relationships on how we feel at
any particular moment, we are in for a rough and rocky journey.
Love is a verb, not a noun. Love is something we do, not something that happens to us.

Stephen Covey tells a great story. On this particular day he had
been presenting a series of talks about proactivity, which is, basi-
cally, the idea that "as human beings we are responsible for our
lives. Our behavior is a function of our decisions, not our conditions. We can subordinate feelings to values. We have the initiative
and the responsibility to make things happen." After his presenta-
tion, Covey was approached by a man who said, "Stephen, I like
what you're saying. But every situation is so different. Look at my
marriage. I'm really worried. My wife and I just don't have the

same feelings for each other we used to have. I guess I just don't love her anymore and she doesn't love me. What can I do?"

"The feeling isn't there anymore?" Covey asked.

"That's right," the man reaffirmed. "And we have three children we're really concerned about. What do you suggest?"

"Love her," Covey replied.

"I told you, the feeling just isn't there anymore."

"Love her."

"You don't understand. The feeling of love just isn't there."

"Then love her. If the feeling isn't there, that's a good reason to love her."

"But how do you love when you don't love?"

"My friend, 'love' is a verb. Love—the feeling—is a fruit of love, the verb. So love her. Serve her. Sacrifice. Listen to her. Empathize. Appreciate. Affirm her. Are you willing to do that?"

Our modern culture equates intimacy with sex and proclaims that love is a feeling. On both counts we are being massively deceived, and we shouldn't allow such misguided philosophies to determine the direction of our lives. Sex is only the shadow of intimacy; feelings are just the aroma of the flower we call love . . . and flowers are not always in bloom.

Love is a choice, and the only truly sensible choice in any situation. Sometimes choosing love means staying together; sometimes it means breaking up. Sometimes choosing love means allowing your child to have what he wants, and sometimes it means denying your child. At times, choosing love means comforting a friend in a difficult situation, while at other times choosing love means telling your friend things she would prefer not to hear.

Love is a choice, and a difficult choice, especially when it means not giving someone what she wants or not telling someone what he wants to hear. Giving people what they want and telling people what they want to hear are easy, compared with choosing love.

Every moment is an opportunity to choose love. The heartache begins when we choose to love and our love is rejected, misunderstood, or, perhaps most painfully, not reciprocated.

You can only choose to love. You cannot determine whether someone else will love you. But if in every situation you choose to love, nothing and no one can ever diminish you. Others may choose not to love you in return, but that doesn't diminish you. Their failure to love is their failure alone and diminishes only themselves.

When you choose not to love, you commit a grave crime against yourself. You may hold back your love to spite another person, or in an attempt to hurt another person. Withholding love is a bit like drinking poison and expecting the other person to die. You may hold back your love in the name of security or safety, but these are only illusions, and in time you will stand as a dwarf compared to the person you could have potentially become if you had chosen love.

Love is a choice. When we choose love, our spirit expands. When we choose not to love, our spirit shrivels.

LOVE CHANGES US

Love is a choice, and an important one, because we become what we love. People who love money become cold and detached. People who love drugs and alcohol become poisonous themselves. When we love others who are selfish and thoughtless we, too, tend to become selfish and thoughtless. And when we love people who are selfless, kind, generous, humble, compassionate, and mindful of the needs of others, we too become selfless, kind, generous, humble, compassionate, and mindful of the needs of others. We become what we love.

What we love intrigues our hearts and captures our imagination. We spend our days thinking about what we love. Thought determines action, actions determine habits, habits determine character, and your character is your destiny. What we love consumes us. It should. Love should be an obsession, but let us remember that we have the power to choose what we become obsessed with.

What are you in love with?

What fascinates you?

What intrigues you and captures your imagination?

Nothing will affect your life more than whom and what you choose to love. Pedro Arrupe explained it in this way. "What you are in love with, what seizes your imagination, will affect everything. It will decide what will get you out of bed in the morning, what you do with your evenings, how you spend your weekends, what you read, who you know, what breaks your heart, and what amazes you with joy and gratitude. Fall in love, stay in love, and it will decide everything."

Love changes us. It should. The very nature of love is transformative. Love is the most powerful agent of change in the universe. We shouldn't fall in love; we should rise in love. Love shouldn't cause us to be some-lesser-version-of-ourselves; love should inspire and challenge us to become the-best-version-of-ourselves. Life is about love, and what we choose to love can transform us for better or for worse.

"I love you just the way you are": these words have echoed around the world for more than twenty-five years in Billy Joel's hit song. And how often people in the midst of an argument say, "Why can't you love me for who I am?"

Should we love people for who they are? Yes. Absolutely. But if we truly love people, we also want them to change.

If you love your wife, you should love and accept her for who she is today, but you should also want her to change and grow, and become the-best-version-of-herself. You should love and accept your children for who they are, but it is natural that you would also want them to continue to grow and change, and explore the range of their potential. You should love and accept your friends for who they are, but you should also be willing to challenge them to change and pursue their essential purpose.

A loving wife says to her husband, "I think you are drinking too much beer and eating too many potato chips while you watch football every Sunday; can I get you something healthier this week when I am at the store?"

"I thought your love was unconditional," the husband replies.

"It's true, I do love you unconditionally," the wife says. "And because I love you, I want you be healthy."

"Why are you trying to change me?" her husband asks. "I thought you loved me just the way I am. Wasn't that our wedding song?"

This dialogue is a constant part of many, many relationships. Conversations like it take place between boyfriends and girlfriends, between husbands and wives, and of course between parents and children. And they always result in a standoff. It may be helpful to ask, What causes the standoff? The answer is that this type of dialogue and standoff are caused when two people don't have a mutual commitment to their essential purpose.

In the example, the wife is trying to help her husband become the-best-version-of-himself, but he is clearly not interested in doing so, at least not in this way. He complains that she is nagging him, and she spends her days wondering how she can ignite his enthusiasm for their relationship again. Their ability to relate is massively hindered because they don't have a mutual commitment to a common purpose.

Love is transformative. Relationships should challenge us to change. They should change the way we see ourselves, the way we see others, and the way we look at the world. But in order for the people we love to feel comfortable with us challenging them to change and grow, we must first agree to make our essential purpose our priority and to pursue it together.

When we explore the seven levels of intimacy in part two of this book, you will discover that it is impossible to achieve this dynamic unless two people can move beyond the third level of intimacy. Intimacy is the key to dynamic change.

WHAT IS LIFE REALLY ALL ABOUT?

M en and women hurry about their daily lives, busying themselves with a million things, and in the midst of all this it is easy to overlook what matters most. Love is the pinnacle of the human experience. The giving and receiving of love is the highest calling of the human person. At first it may seem that the giving of love is the difficult part, but for many of us, opening our hearts to receive the love of others can be the greater challenge.

We should busy ourselves with giving and receiving love. And as we can only control the giving, and not the receiving, we should order our lives so that we are preoccupied with giving love wherever we go and to whomever we meet.

Certainly we must work and pay our bills and study and pass our exams. All these things we do in order to survive, but love is what we survive for.

What's important to you?

What matters most?

How are you spending your one short life?

When your time is done, who do you want to remember you?

How do you want to be remembered?

If your life were over tomorrow, what would be left undone? Unsaid?

What is life really all about?

Life is not about what sort of shoes you wear. Life isn't about whether or not you live on the right street, or whether you live in a big, fancy house. Life's not about what sort of car you drive. It's not about what football team you cheer for. It's not about whether your football team wins. It's not about whether you made the football team, or might make the football team, or what position you might have on the football team. Life's not about what college you went to, or might go to, or what college your kids might go to. Life is not about these things.

Life's not about money. Life is not about what sort of position or what sort of power you have. It's not about whether you're famous. It's not about whether or not you vacation in all the right places every year. Life's not about what sort of clothes you wear and whether they have fancy labels that massively increase their price. Life is not about these things.

Life's not about who you've dated or who you're dating. Life's not about who your parents are or whom you know. Life's not even about what sort of grades you get in school; your parents and your teachers don't want me to tell you that, but it's true. Life is not about these things.

Life is about love. It's about whom you love and whom you hurt. Life's about how you love yourself and how you hurt yourself. Life's about how you love and hurt the people close to you. Life is about how you love and hurt the people who just cross your path for a moment.

Life is about love.

PART TWO

◦⁊⁊⁊⊙

How the Seven Levels of Intimacy Will Change Your Relationships . . . and Your Life!

Intimacy Is a Legitimate Need

There are some things we want just because we want them, and there are some things we want because we need them. Intimacy is a need. You cannot live long without food to eat and water to drink, and it would all be over in a matter of minutes without air to breathe. Food to eat, water to drink, and air to breathe are legitimate needs. So is intimacy. You can survive without it. But you cannot thrive and become the-best-version-of-yourself.

There is a restlessness within each of us that wants to be calmed, tamed. This restlessness is our heart's yearning for intimacy. In our efforts to feel complete, worthy, fulfilled, and contented, we often chase pleasure, possessions, and achievement. We convince ourselves that if we can experience the right type of pleasure, amass enough possessions, or attain certain accomplishments, the restlessness will be overcome and we will finally have a sense of fulfillment and contentment. But while each encounter with pleasure, possessions, and achievement can be very satisfying for the brief moment they are experienced in, the aftermath of these experiences leaves us yearning for something more.

So we chase more intense pleasures, larger piles of possessions, and grander achievements, mistakenly believing that this time we will find fulfillment. But we don't, and in the absence of another path, we repeat the process over and over and over again, until we die. We remain restless until the end. We continue to subscribe to the myth that pleasure, possessions, and achievement will fulfill us. Yet after each encounter we are left with the same dissatisfied aftertaste.

Why?

You simply never can get enough of what you don't really need.

What is it that we really need?

We don't need more money, faster cars, bigger houses, or grander promotions. The human person needs one thing above all else: intimacy.

We continue to chase our illegitimate wants and neglect our legitimate needs. The result is that we live in restless discontent. Contentment is to be found only by creating a lifestyle that tends to our legitimate needs, physical, emotional, intellectual, and spiritual. Intimacy is one of our real and legitimate needs, and all the pleasures, possessions, and achievements on the planet will not satisfy you as the fulfillment of your legitimate needs will. The mutual fulfilling of legitimate needs is the pinnacle of relationships. This is what it means to be soul mates.

Do you ever get the feeling that something is wrong, or that something is missing in your life? Do you ever get the sense that there must be more to life?

Something is wrong.
Something is missing.
There is more.
Intimacy.

THE SEVEN LEVELS AT A GLANCE

The seven levels of intimacy will change the way you look at relationships every day. Each level will help you to recognize certain signs in your relationships and empower you to embrace intimacy.

The first level of intimacy is the level of clichés.

The second level of intimacy is the level of facts.

The third level of intimacy is the level of opinions.

The fourth level of intimacy is the level of hopes and dreams.

The fifth level of intimacy is the level of feelings.

The sixth level of intimacy is the level of faults, fears, and failures.

The seventh level of intimacy is the level of legitimate needs.

The journey through the seven levels is a journey from the shallow to the deep, from the irrelevant to the relevant, from illegitimate desires to legitimate needs, from judgment to acceptance, from fear to courage, from false self to true self, from loneliness to profound companionship, and from isolation to unity.

NAVIGATING THE SEVEN LEVELS

The seven levels of intimacy is a model. The model doesn't live and breathe, as you and the people you love do. It's a model, and models are imperfect. But models are also brilliant, powerful, and deeply meaningful. A bit like people, I suppose.

Models are powerful because they simplify the most complex situations that we encounter in our lives and allow us to see them with clarity, so that they can be understood.

The seven levels of intimacy is a model. It is not perfect, but it is powerful and deeply meaningful, and it will change forever the way you view your relationships. There are a handful of models that have changed the way we see the world or various aspects of our lives. The supply-and-demand model changed the way we view economics. Before anyone believed that the world was round, someone had to present a model. Powerful models have been changing the way we see the world and live our lives from the beginning, and I feel certain that the seven levels of intimacy will change forever the way you view the world of relationships.

Effective models are simple and practical, and their accuracy can be corroborated through our everyday experience of the subject presented in the model. In this case the subject is relationships, in particular intimacy, and you will be able to see the model at work in your relationships daily. If a model is to be effective and useful, you must know and understand the rules that govern it. The second part of this book is dedicated to learning about the model of the seven levels of intimacy.

These are the rules and guidelines that govern the model.

1. Relationships are rarely confined to any single level. For example, it is a mistake to identify a relationship as a fifth-level relationship or a third-level relationship. Your relationships will experience many of the seven levels every day. The only exceptions to this rule are casual secondary relationships, such as the relationship you may have with a grocery store clerk or a bank teller. It is possible for such a relationship to be confined to the first level of

intimacy. We will discuss this in detail in the next chapter—in fact, all of these rules will make much more sense to you once you have read the chapter relating to each of the levels of intimacy. With that in mind, you may wish to come back and reread these rules and guidelines after you have finished chapter thirteen.

2.   The seven levels of intimacy are not a task to be completed and graduate from. You don't gaze into each other's eyes one day and say, "Hey, we're in the seventh level." You may experience the seventh level, and I hope you do, but that doesn't mean the job is done and you can fall back into the lethargy, distraction, and indifference that destroy most relationships. We move in and out of the different levels of intimacy in our relationships everyday. Nor do you sit up one day and say, "We reached the fourth level yesterday; let's do the fifth level today." The seven levels are not necessarily experienced in order. This will also make more sense once you learn about the seven levels in the coming chapters. But it is important for you to be aware of these dynamics before we embark on our exploration of the seven levels.

3.   It is also important to know that not all relationships deserve to experience all seven levels of intimacy, nor are they meant to. Some relationships belong in the first level of intimacy, and only the first level of intimacy. Other relationships may be worthy of all seven levels of intimacy, but to varying degrees. There may be some things that are appropriate to share with your sister that are not appropriate to share with a colleague at work. There may be intimacies that belong in a relationship between a husband and a wife, but not in a relationship between a parent and a child. But our primary relationship should be a place where we can experience the depths of intimacy. There should be no limits to what we are willing to explore here, unless of course it will hurt the other person in

a way that will not help him or her to become the-best-version-of-himself (or herself).

4. You cannot rush intimacy. You cannot force the seven levels; these things don't happen on a timetable, nor are they rigid. The process is liquid and ever changing. Certainly, intimacy requires effort, but the attainment of intimacy is a little like geology, the study of time and pressure. In this case, the gentle pressure is the effort of you and your partner.

Models have rules. That's what makes them work. These are the few and simple rules necessary to understand the seven levels of intimacy.

The best way to learn something is to teach it. So, as you move through the seven levels, discuss them with your partner, your friends, your family, and your colleagues. Discussing them (and certainly explaining them to others) will increase your understanding of each level and of the model in general.

Know the model, share the model, and it will transform your relationships.

IDENTIFY THREE RELATIONSHIPS

One very significant piece of feedback that I have received when I have presented the seven levels of intimacy as part of my seminars and retreats is that every level tends to bring to mind particular relationships. This is very natural and normal, but in order to get the most out of your first reading of the seven levels, I encourage you to identify between one to three relationships that you would like to focus on for the next seven chapters.

The reason is that some of us have a tendency to focus on the positive and some of us have a tendency to focus on the negative. This being the case, it is very easy for us to focus on a different relationship for each of the seven levels (from either a positive or a negative point of view) and never really take a good, long, hard, honest look at any single relationship.

Take a few moments now to identify which relationships you would most like to look at in relation to the seven levels. You may wish to focus entirely on your primary relationship the first time you read through the seven levels, and that is fine. Or you may wish to look at a variety of relationships. If you have a primary relationship, include it as one of your three, even if you consider it your best relationship and it is thriving. Don't choose more than three relationships to focus on during your first reading of the seven levels; doing so defeats the purpose and will dilute the effectiveness. And choose different types of relationships. For example, if your wife has just died and you don't have a significant other at this point in your life, don't choose three of your children, even if your relationships with them are the three that you most want to work on. Choose one of your children and a sibling or a friend. Similarly, if you are young and single, don't choose three of your sisters. A variety of relationships will help you to understand the breadth and depth of the seven levels of intimacy, and perhaps more important, will help you to understand yourself and the way you relate in a much more comprehensive way. So choose three relationships to focus on and write your choices down now; then, at the end of the section about each level, evaluate each of the relationships you have chosen in terms of that level of intimacy.

In time, you may wish to go through the seven levels again with another relationship or relationships in mind. You may also wish to reread the seven levels with the same relationships in mind; this will show you how much certain relationships have changed and grown since you first read this book. For this reason, I encourage you to take some notes as you move through the seven levels. That way, the next time you read through you will be able to compare your notes and assess where your relationships have grown.

The seven levels of intimacy will revolutionize the way you experience relationships. The model empowers us, gives us a map, shows us where we are and where we are going. The seven levels of intimacy model will give you the courage to rise above your fears, by showing you why we act in certain ways and what the rewards of facing our relationship fears are. Educated and empowered, you will then be willing to explore the deep places of intimacy with the people you love and want to love more.

CHAPTER SEVEN

꧁

CLICHÉS: THE FIRST LEVEL OF INTIMACY

IS YOUR RELATIONSHIP A CLICHÉ?

A cliché is a trite phrase or expression, or the idea expressed by it; a hackneyed theme, characterization, or situation; something that has become overly familiar and commonplace (Webster's Dictionary). Has your relationship become a cliché?

The first level of intimacy is the level of clichés. At this level we engage in casual interactions, encounters that reveal little about each person and rely on fleeting and superficial exchanges. If a social encounter doesn't move beyond an exchange of clichés, it is not even worthy of being called a conversation. This style of communicating is very useful in becoming acquainted with a person and in the day-to-day transactions of our lives, but relationships are not transactions. Transactions are boring and monotonous, like clichés. Relationships should be dynamic collaborations. So, while the first level of intimacy is good for establishing a connection with people, and necessary for conducting the daily affairs of our lives, clichés can destroy the soul of a relationship. Thus they can prevent any true intimacy.

We all have relationships on the cliché level. The dialogue in these relationships tends to go something like this:

"How are you?"

"Fine."

"How was your day?"

"Great."

"What did you do?"

"Same as yesterday!"

Now, if you communicate with the man who bags your groceries only with clichés, that is one thing, but if cliché is the way you communicate with your spouse or your teenage child, that is something entirely different.

Is your primary relationship becoming a cliché? Is it becoming trite? Transactional? Has it become overly familiar, to the point of being disrespectful? Has it become commonplace? If it has, don't despair.

WHY DO WE COMMUNICATE IN CLICHÉS?

We communicate in clichés for a myriad of reasons. Some of these reasons are simple and valid, while others are tremendously complex.

The simplest and most valid reason is that clichés are powerful in helping us make initial connections with people and in helping us to maintain a connection with people at a certain level. Asking someone, "How are you?" is perhaps the simplest and most common way to begin a conversation. Making that person feel that you are actually interested in hearing the answer is the key to intimacy. Let's face it, when most people ask, "How are you?" they are just being polite and they expect you to reply in cliché form by saying, "Fine!" or "Great!" Clichés are great conversation starters, but if they don't lead anywhere over time they become shallow and superficial, and they fail to quench our thirst for intimacy.

At the same time, a cliché can be used to kill a conversation. Those who are indifferent, selfish, or afraid become experts at employing the cliché to destroy any chance of meaningful communication. For example, a wife may ask her husband, "What did you think of what happened in Europe today?" and he replies, "It is what it is!" Another example might be a father trying to begin a discussion with his teenage child by asking, "Do you still feel like you can come and talk to your mother and me?" The child replies, "Whatever!" On paper these conversations seem harsh and rude, but they are becoming commonplace in more and more relationships that are perceived by the outside world as being functioning, healthy, and normal. I assure you, such exchanges are anything but functioning, healthy, and normal. They are a sign of deeply fractured relationships that are desperately in need of attention.

The young people of today have perfected this form of communication and transmuted it into a form of noncommunication, with the creation of clichés such as "What's up?" and "Whatever!" It is also interesting to note that teens usually use clichés to avoid deeper levels of communication with the adults in their lives, and that they communicate very differently with friends within their peer group.

Why do so many teenagers communicate in this way with most of the adults in their life? Sometimes it is because they feel that if they do communicate in any meaningful way they will be judged or criticized. They sense that they will not be accepted for who they are. Perhaps they communicate in this way because they feel that nobody understands them, and most are unwilling to try. Others may resort to the constant use of clichés to communicate because they believe (consciously or subconsciously) that every-thing within them is worthless and pathetic. Some are lazy and in-different to others. Still others are so completely self-absorbed that they find communicating with others to be boring and a waste of time.

The reasons adults have are startlingly similar. We are afraid of being judged and criticized. We sense that we are not accepted and are afraid of being rejected. We feel that nobody understands us and that most people are more interested in being understood themselves than they are in trying to understand us. Secretly we all carry with us a shame, and at times believe that we are worthless and pathetic. We are lazy. We are indifferent. We are self-absorbed.

Clichés are safe. We cling to them for that reason. But when they are overused in a relationship that deserves to enjoy greater depth of intimacy, clichés keep us at arm's length from the one thing we cannot live happily without.

INCAPABLE OF SMALL TALK

In other relationships, we encounter the opposite of this cliché-dominated communication. With everything that is good, abuses exist at both extremes. Some people abuse the first level of intimacy by using clichés too much, while others abuse it by using cliché communication too little or refusing to engage in small talk at all. This kind of behavior is equally harsh, abrupt, rude, and in-sensitive.

Imagine a person incapable of small talk. You probably don't have to imagine; you probably know someone who fits this de-scription. They seem incapable of being cordial and polite, inca-pable of regular social interactions. They may be abrupt and arrogant in their manner, quiet and distant to all onlookers, and when they do speak they come off as harsh, because they don't ease into a conversation. They cut straight to the topics and big issues (or at least, what they consider to be the big issues), which usually revolve around their own area of expertise. If you try to call them on this, they will explain that they simply cannot "humor fools" and that nothing is gained from small talk.

We must ask: Does this attitude and approach encourage intimacy? The answer is, of course, a resounding no. In fact, such people in many ways resemble the teenager whose answer to everything is "Whatever." These are often men and women of towering intellect, but they hide behind that intellect. Others who employ this tactic are not intellectual giants, but create some other mask to assert their superiority. Why? They have all the same reasons any of us do for avoiding intimacy, but mostly, they fear it, though it is the one thing they cannot live happily without. It is this fear that drives them from the world of others and into the world of self. And in that world of self they begin the narcissistic obsession and eventually convince themselves that others are boring and a waste of time. As the years pass in this world of self, they become indifferent to the interests and needs of others, and incapable of the simplest of human communications and considerations. They may claim that their genius prevents them from thinking about the trivial, because their minds are constantly occupied with grander and loftier ideas, but the truth is they lack the common decency to ask another human being: How are you? How was your day? What did you do? and the empathy to listen and care.

They will tell you that they are simply incapable of small talk, as if they were born this way. The truth is they have chosen to be incapable of small talk. The bottom line is that such people are scared to death. They may seem awkward in social situations, unable to engage with people, but this disposition is the fruit of years of effort. We are all able to make people feel welcome and accepted, by taking an interest in them. We become good at this the same way we become good at anything, with practice.

We all find ways to avoid intimacy. Some of those ways are highly sophisticated, while others are simple and transparent. But the effect is the same: we continue to yearn for our fill of intimacy.

CAREFREE TIMELESSNESS

One thing can help you move beyond the tyranny of the cliché level more effectively than anything else: *carefree timelessness*. What is carefree timelessness? It is time together. Not five or ten minutes, but two hours or four hours, or a weekend away. And it *isn't* just a lot of time together. Carefree timelessness is time together without an agenda.

All relationships thrive under the condition of carefree timelessness, but we don't gift our relationships with carefree timelessness. We try to shove them into five minutes here and ten minutes there, a cell phone call here and an instant message there. Do we actually expect that our relationships can genuinely thrive under these conditions? Do we sincerely feel that this is enough to form a significant connection with another human being? Or have we simply failed to think about it, because we are distracted by the everyday insanity of our busy lives?

If you want your teenage child to open up to you a little more, spend an afternoon together without an agenda. Do something different together. Make this a regular part of your relationship. The first time, your teenager will be understandably suspicious, but once this becomes a normal part of your lives together he or she will sense your genuine interest and will begin to open up.

The same approach can be taken with any relationship. Simply add some carefree timelessness and watch it begin to grow and thrive.

Think back to when your primary relationship began. You probably spent a lot of time together, and when you weren't together you probably spent a lot of time thinking about the next time you would be together. Was there spontaneity and carefree timelessness in your relationship at the beginning? How much energy did you put into trying to please each other?

You may think that you spend more time together today, but do you really, or are you simply in the same place together more of the time? The world is full of people living together alone. Is there always an agenda when you do spend time together? When was the last time you woke up with absolutely nothing planned and said to each other, "What would you like to do today?" Or perhaps you simply stopped trying to please each other somewhere along the way. Did you? When did you stop trying to please her? And why? Don't you miss the happiness you found in making someone else happy?

We all want to have great relationships, but we get distracted. We all want to experience times of carefree timelessness, but we get preoccupied with and distracted by all the urgent things.

Every morning when you wake up, you face a list of urgent things to do. Your list of urgent things might be in your planner or on your desk; it might be on your fridge or on your computer. Your list of urgent things might be in your mind, it might be in your spouse's mind! But every day there's that list. We rush around endlessly doing all these urgent things, and if we are not careful we will rush around doing urgent things for the rest of our lives.

The problem is, the most important things are hardly ever urgent.

When was the last time you woke up and said to yourself, "I urgently have to work out today"? You don't urgently have to work out; you have to skip your workout because you have urgent things to do. When was the last time you said to your assistant, "Cancel all my meetings. I urgently need to read a good book that will fuel my mind, expand my vision of myself and the world, and intellectually stimulate me"? When was the last time you thought, "What I really need to do urgently today is go down to Wild Oats and get myself some fresh organic fruits and vegetables and make myself a truly great meal that will genuinely fuel and energize my body"? You don't urgently need to eat a good meal; you urgently need to go to the drive-through.

The most important things are hardly ever urgent.

In each of the four areas of life (physical, emotional, intellectual, and spiritual) we know what is most important, but we tell ourselves that we will attend to those matters later, when we have finished with the urgent things. "I'll do it when I get caught up!" we tell others and ourselves. This might not be so much of a problem if we did actually do the most important things when we got caught up. But we don't. Not because we don't want to, but because we never get caught up. Seriously, when was the last time you sat down and you said to yourself, "I'm caught up now!"

It doesn't happen. Your to-do list just gets longer and longer every day. You never get caught up; you just get more and more behind every day. Some days you feel as if your life has a momentum of its own, as if it would go on with or without you. "Caught up"! Who are we kidding?

Because the most important things are hardly ever urgent, that is why we have to place them at the center of our lives. We have to put them on our schedules, because if we don't we simply won't get around to them. "Things which matter most must never be at the mercy of things which matter least" was Goethe's advice.

We have to make carefree timelessness a priority.

The experts at carefree timelessness are, of course, teenagers.

While they may use clichés to avoid intimacy with many of the adults in their lives, in relating to their friends in their peer group they have perfected the art of carefree timelessness.

What do teenagers do? They talk on the phone. How long do they talk on the phone for? Hours. Johnny has been on the phone for four hours and when he gets off the phone his father asks, "How long have you been on the phone?"

"Not long, " Johnny replies.

"Who were you talking to?" his mother asks.

"Susan," Johnny replies. Susan is Johnny's girlfriend.

"What did you two talk about?" his father asks now.

And what does Johnny say?

"Nothing!"

Carefree timelessness!

When Johnny said, "Not long!" he wasn't necessarily telling a lie. When he told his parents, "Nothing!" he wasn't necessarily being evasive. The nature of carefree timelessness is to be timeless. You lose track of time. Carefree timelessness is carefree. It has nothing to achieve other than the enjoyment of each other's company.

Teenagers are experts at it. How often do parents ask, when their children are going out with friends, "Where are you going?" The children reply, "I don't know!" Of course, we consider this an unacceptable answer, but it may just be the truth.

Carefree timelessness. It is the reason young people fall in love so easily. The lack of carefree timelessness is the reason the rest of us fall out of love so easily. Carefree timelessness causes us to fall in love with life and others, and it will help you move your relationships beyond the first level of intimacy.

The question is: How do we go about it?

Whether you decide you need some carefree timelessness with your spouse, your boyfriend or girlfriend, your children or parents, or your friends and colleagues, there are a thousand ways to create it.

The first thing you need to do is schedule it. Now I hear that objection in the back of your mind. You are thinking, if I have to schedule it then it's not carefree timelessness. Not so. Think back to our definition of carefree timelessness, as time spent together without an agenda. I didn't say that it is unscheduled and will happen all on its own. We know it won't. We have to schedule it, but we don't need an agenda.

Let me give you an example of carefree timelessness. If you said to your wife, "Let's plan to spend Friday afternoon together next week, and we will just decide what we want to do when it comes around." That's time together, with no agenda: carefree timelessness.

On the other hand, suppose you said to your wife, "Let's plan to spend Friday afternoon together next week, and we can stop by the store and buy that new television, return those trousers you bought me that didn't fit, have lunch, pick up the kids, and then come home and finish raking those leaves." It is certainly time together, but it also sounds anything but carefree.

Do you need some carefree timelessness with your significant other?

There are a thousand ways to spend your carefree timelessness. Nobody needs help with that; you schedule the time together, and when the time arrives you simply turn to each other and ask, "What would you like to do?"

If you have the drive and discipline to make carefree timelessness a habit in your primary relationship, you will be stunned and amazed by how powerfully it changes your life together. Make it a habit.

Two hours once a week.

One whole day once a month.

A weekend getaway once a quarter.

Give it a try, then send me an e-mail in three months and tell me how much it has changed your relationship.

Our lives as individuals change when our habits change. It's not freak luck that changes our lives, and God doesn't have any favorites. Our relationships change when our habits as members of those relationships change. Make carefree timelessness a habit in your primary relationship. And as you begin to be convinced of its power, make it a habit in all of your high-level relationships.

I have powerful memories of carefree timelessness with both my mother and my father as I was growing up. I have seven brothers; and it would be easy to think that in that type of environment siblings just get lost in the crowd. Not so—at least, not in my family. Both my mother and my father went out of their way to make sure that we had the individual nurturing we needed to grow into confident young men. My visits to the Art Gallery of New South Wales with my mother were one example of this individual carefree timelessness my parents lavished upon my brothers and me. The gallery had an exceptional permanent collection and attracted world-class traveling exhibits. Renoir, Van Gogh, Monet, Picasso, Warhol, Matisse, Pollock, and many, many, others were introduced to me by my mother inside the walls of that gallery. It was there that I developed my fascination with great art and with the artists behind the masterpieces.

After we visited the gallery we would have lunch and talk, just me and my mother. It seemed natural and normal to confide in my mother my hopes and dreams, and to speak about the happenings of my life. We had carefree timelessness. My father was at home with my brothers. Today was my day. My brothers would each have their day in turn. As I think back on it I am not sure how often we had such days, perhaps only once a year, but they left a powerful impression upon me.

Do you need some carefree timelessness with your children?

Millions of people confine important relationships to the first level of intimacy. They communicate primarily in clichés because they often sense that nobody is really interested in them and that nobody cares. Studies show that on average a parent spends less than seventeen minutes in conversation with their teenage child each week. Is it any wonder that we have trouble understanding their world?

In a culture obsessed with the value of time, one of the real and tangible ways for us to let people know that we care, that we are interested in trying to know them, is to give them our time. Not grudgingly and stingily, but lavishly. Love is generous and abundant. By lavishing our time upon the people we love, we demonstrate that we love them, that we care about them, and that we are willing to make an effort to know and be known.

Carefree timelessness is the key to moving beyond the first level of intimacy, out of the impersonal world of clichés and into the world of personal conversation. In fact, the lesson of carefree timelessness plays a significant role in all seven levels of intimacy. Give the gift of carefree timelessness to your significant other, to your children, to your parents, to everyone with whom you have a high-level relationship. Give the people you love the gift of carefree timelessness. It will transform them, and you, and the relationships you share. Then and only then, restored once more by that carefree timelessness, together, will you discover the lightheartedness essential to the thriving we were given this life to enjoy.

All great things can only be achieved with a light heart. Lightheartedness is the fruit of carefree timelessness.

CHAPTER EIGHT

❦

FACTS: THE SECOND LEVEL OF INTIMACY

WHO'S THAT HIDING BEHIND THE FACTS?

The second level of intimacy is the level of facts. At this level, we tend to focus our communication on the facts about our lives and the world we live in. These facts could include everything from the happenings of our day to the events we read about in the newspaper. We stick to the facts in the second level. They are mundane, and in most cases self-evident, so they generally don't create conflict. As a result, we perceive the facts to be very safe; as we perceive clichés to be safe. What do they keep us safe from? The daunting idea of intimacy.

If a relationship is confined to this second level of intimacy, we talk about the weather, sports, how the stock market is performing, and what we did today. These conversations tend to be in staccato form. The questions and the answers are normally very brief, usually just a series of one-liners. We simply ask:

"How was your day?"

"Fine!"

"What did you do?"

"I went to work. At lunchtime I went to see Dr. Jones about my knee. I saw Mrs. Miller at the bank and stopped by to see Grandma. Did you know her cat has run away?"

The first question and answer ("How was your day?" "Fine!") was on the cliché level and was used to initiate a conversation. This is the proper use of the first level of intimacy. The second question ("What did you do?") could have met with a clichéd answer, "Same old stuff," which would have shut down the conversation. Perhaps not immediately, but most people will only ask so many questions, and receive so many clichéd answers, before they give up their hope of a conversation. It is in this way that we so often use clichés to stonewall intimacy. But in the example at hand, the speaker leads into the second level of intimacy by replying to the question ("What did you do?") with a litany of facts. The facts were impersonal, but this conversation did progress beyond the mere exchange of clichés and into the second level of intimacy.

It is also important to note that this reply ends with a question ("Did you know her cat has run away?"), opening the opportunity for further discussion. Nonetheless, this conversation is simply a recitation of impersonal facts and observations.

The facts would have been personal if she had said,

"I went to work, and I am really excited about this new project I am working on." This is no longer just a statement of impersonal fact, as it reveals how she feels about work.

"At lunchtime I went to see Dr. Jones about my knee. She keeps telling me it's healing. But it's been six months, and I don't know if she knows what she's talking about." This statement moves beyond the facts, revealing something about the speaker through her opinion.

"I saw Mrs. Miller at the bank; we only need twelve hundred

dollars now before we can take that cruise." This tells you something about the speaker's hopes and dreams.

"And did I tell you I saw Grandma? She is distraught because her cat ran away. She was so sad and I felt so helpless." This goes far beyond mere facts, telling you that the speaker is concerned about others and is capable of being empathetic.

The second level of intimacy (facts), like its predecessor (clichés), is very useful in forming an initial acquaintance with a person, but if we remain in the level of nonpersonal facts for too long, the relationship becomes stale. After a while, the recital of impersonal facts becomes boring and monotonous, and all great relationships are dynamic collaborations. Far from being boring and monotonous, they are creative and exciting.

We all have relationships in which we communicate exclusively with impersonal facts. Your relationship with a financial adviser may be strictly professional, confined to the pleasantries and facts of the first two levels of intimacy. In some relationships that is appropriate, but in our high-level relationships that is deeply inappropriate. Are any of your high-level relationships being held hostage by impersonal facts?

OUR NATURAL CURIOSITY AND LOVE OF LEARNING

One of the redeeming qualities of facts is that they have the potential to stimulate us intellectually, to arouse our natural curiosity, and to teach us to fall in love with learning. Some facts are, of course, better in this way than others. What determines which facts are better? Everything makes sense in relation to our essential purpose. It follows, then, that facts that help you become the-best-version-of-yourself are better than those that do not.

Suppose you are at a dinner party and everyone is talking about someone who is having an affair. It seems self-evident that this conversation (whether the affair is fact or fiction) is unlikely to help anyone become the-best-version-of-himself or herself. We may respond to this conversation by renewing our internal commitment to be faithful to our partner, but that would be making the best of a bad situation.

On the other hand, suppose you are at a dinner party and someone is talking about a trip he took to Paris, his visit to the Picasso Museum, and a book he has been reading about Picasso's life. It is possible that even though the conversation involves nothing more than the exchange of facts, it would be helping you to become the-best-version-of-yourself. How? The content in itself is more intellectually stimulating. But, more important, if you were to embark on a discussion of Picasso's life and his personal struggle to overcome his inner conflicts, you would move the conversation up another level.

Every conversation can move you closer to the-best-version-of-yourself or lead you away from your essential purpose. We therefore have an enormous responsibility every time we engage in a conversation with anyone. Before we open our mouths, we should ask ourselves: Is what I am about to say going to help this person (or these people) become the-best-version-of-himself or herself?

One of the great virtues of the second level of intimacy is that it has the potential to ignite our love of learning. For many of us, the love of learning is trained out of us when we are very young. We tend to associate learning with schools, assignments, exams, and report cards. Textbooks, overburdened with a myriad facts that seem irrelevant to our lives, create a negative perception regarding books in general. We go to school, take our exams, and receive graduation certificates, but few are really ignited with a genuine love of learning. Cramming for exams destroys the natural human curiosity so evident in young children, who ask a million questions and meet every answer with "Why?" The human mind is naturally curious, wants to grow and expand, but too often our modern educational systems rob us of this natural love of learning in their quest to graduate us.

Conversations will very often go where we choose to take them. The conversations that take place on the second level of intimacy are an opportunity to reawaken our natural yearning for knowledge and to reengage the curiosity that may have been asleep in you since shortly after you began structured education. Your mind delights in learning new things. Feed your mind. Your mind needs a diet, just as your body needs a diet: not a diet that deprives you, but one that fuels you.

Most people are in possession of rare facts and insights into certain topics; we have to learn to engage them in a discussion about these topics. As we venture through the remaining five levels of intimacy, we are going to learn how to engage people in conversations about the things they are passionate about and the topics they possess expertise in. This will empower us to transform almost any conversation from a mundane and boring exchange of facts into a fascinating and intellectually stimulating discussion.

We move from the second to the third level of intimacy in two steps. The first step is to move from lower-level impersonal facts to higher-level impersonal facts. Lower-level impersonal facts concern current events, the weather, and the results of the market. Conversations concerned with higher-level impersonal facts might include a discussion of the life of Abraham Lincoln or Mahatma Gandhi, what causes a tsunami to occur, or the reasons Google continues to confound stock analysts. This is the first step, from lower level to higher-level impersonal facts. In the second step, we move from impersonal to personal facts; this is the bridge that takes us into the third level of intimacy. We will discuss it shortly, but first a look at the power of speech and how we use (and abuse) this power in our everyday lives.

THE POWER OF SPEECH

As I have traveled the globe in recent years I have had a couple of very scary moments. I was sitting in a restaurant late one night, after a talk in Cork, Ireland. We were the last customers and I was just finishing some chocolate ice cream when two men carrying sawn-off shotguns and wearing balaclavas over their faces burst through the door. One went to the cash register and the other pointed his gun straight at my friends and me.

An experience like that certainly makes you think about your life. I was seriously scared again during a visit to Chicago a couple of years ago, when I lost my voice. I had spent the day visiting three high schools and had strained my vocal cords, but I was afraid I wouldn't get my voice back. You see, I love to speak. I cannot imagine having this message within me and not being able to share it.

Imagine that you wake up tomorrow morning and can no longer speak. Imagine the inconvenience of the simplest tasks. Imagine how much more difficult it would be to relate to the people you love. Imagine how you would yearn to speak. Imagine how irritated you might be with people who waste their words, or refuse to speak their love even though they are able to.

Speech is one of the most powerful gifts the human person possesses, and like most of our gifts it can be used positively, to raise people up, or negatively, to pull people down. Words are either positively or negatively charged. Let's take a look at some of the ways we use our power of speech every day.

CATCH SOMEONE DOING THE RIGHT THING

Recently during a stay at a Hilton hotel, I was struck by a slogan on the customer comment cards: "Catch Someone Doing the Right Thing!" Too often we only catch people doing the wrong thing. Not because they never do the right thing, but because we are more likely to speak out when something isn't the way we like it than when it is. We are more likely to speak out when things go wrong than we are when things go right. We expect things to go right, and we take them for granted when they do.

Think back to a time when someone caught you doing something right. How did it make you feel? When was the last time you caught someone doing something right and praised that person for his or her efforts?

As we grow in emotional maturity, we realize that everyone needs encouragement. When we shower our praise upon others, we energize them. Whom will you energize with your praise today?

RASH JUDGMENT

A couple of summers ago, I was in an ice cream shop with some friends. We were sitting around talking and enjoying our ice cream when a woman with four children came in. The children then proceed to rip around the store, screaming and shouting and generally causing mayhem and disruption. At first I tried to ignore them, but it was impossible. My friends and I eventually just sat there and looked at each other in disbelief. But the thing that really got to me was that the mother seemed completely oblivious to the actions of her children and the disruption they were causing. Finally, I couldn't contain myself. Standing up, I walked over to where she was sitting and said, "Ma'am, don't you think you should at least try to control your children?" Looking up at me in a daze, and then at them, she said, "I'm so sorry. We just left the hospital. Their father died about an hour ago and I don't think they know how to deal with it, and I just have all these thoughts running through my mind. I'm not sure I know how to deal with it, either."

How do you think I felt? How quickly we rush to judge people and situations. But we judge them from where we sit, from our situation, circumstances, and experience of life. And everything looks different depending on where you look at it from.

It is easy to get into the habit of judgment. Once we begin to judge people, things, and circumstances, judgment can rule our inner and outer dialogues. An inner dialogue (the mental conversation we are constantly having with ourselves) of judgment creates nothing but restlessness and discontent. An outer dialogue of judgment destroys honest and open communication, because none of us want to make ourselves vulnerable if we sense we will be shot down by judgment.

For the next twenty-four hours, try not to judge a single person or situation. Give people the benefit of the doubt. Try to see the situation from where they sit. Practice non-judgment. Non-judgment fosters open and honest communication and breeds intimacy. Judgment is death to intimacy.

Judgment is one of the great poisons that kill relationships. Begin each day with this affirmation: "Today I shall judge nothing that occurs." When you do find yourself judging people, places, things, circumstances, gently repeat the simple mantra, "Today I shall judge nothing that occurs."

You may very quickly find that both your inner and outer dialogue are littered with judgments. When I first tried this exercise, I was astounded and humbled by how many judgments enter into my heart and mind in the course of a single day. If this is what you discover, it may be helpful to break the day down into hours, repeating the mantra each and every hour: "For the next hour I will not judge anything that occurs."

The ability to suspend judgment is an essential characteristic if we wish to explore the very depths of intimacy. The path that leads to intimacy is blocked to those who are unwilling or unable to practice nonjudgment.

CRITICISM AND CORRECTION

My eldest brother, Mark, is a national executive with a supermarket chain in Australia. Many years ago, he was managing a large store in the Melbourne area; one day, he was showing me around and we were discussing business models that are based on enormous volume and tiny profit margins. As we wandered through the store we came across a teenager who was stocking the shelves. I noticed my brother look and then look again, and then he turned to me and said, "Excuse me a minute, Matthew. Could you wait at the end of the aisle for me?"

As I walked away, I heard my brother masterfully tell the young man that he wasn't packing the shelf properly. And then he got down on his hands and knees in the aisle, unpacked that portion of the shelf, and demonstrated how to do it properly. All the while, he was saying things like "You're not in trouble"; "I'm not mad at you"; "Someone had to show me how to do this once." Then Mark had the boy pack the other half of the space as he had just taught. Before he moved on, my brother asked the teenager how he was doing at school, which team he thought would win the football championship this year, and how his family was doing.

I learned a powerful lesson that day. Mark is a master with people; his patience is rare and extremely valuable. And his correction wasn't judgmental and didn't come across as critical. He didn't just walk past and say, "That looks like crap!" or "Are you stupid? You're doing that wrong!" That would have been destructive; Mark chose to build his employee up rather than tearing him down. He had to tear part of his employee's work down, but he didn't have to tear the person down.

There is a difference between correction and criticism.

Mark chose to correct his employee in a way that was instructional, practical, and devoid of ego. When the manager of a multimillion-dollar store is on his hands and knees in the middle of aisle nine, it's not about ego. Mark reminded the young man that we all have to be taught things at some point. He sent me to wait at a distance because "you should never correct an employee in front of other people," he told me later. "Why?" I asked. "It dents their pride, and pride is blinding. Once you have them thinking about their pride, their response is going to be pride-driven."

The real genius was that Mark didn't allow the correction to be a conversation unto itself. He used it to connect personally with one of his employees by progressing from the correction into a brief personal chat.

I have seen my brother exercise this same patience with some of my younger brothers as well as with his own children. It is something I have been trying long and hard to reproduce in my own life. The art of correcting people without producing a battle of egos is a valuable tool in relationships.

THE VENOM OF GOSSIP

One of the most negative manifestations of the second level of intimacy is gossip. Gossip is defined as a trifling, an often groundless rumor, usually of a personal, sensational, or intimate nature, or just plain idle talk that casts aspersions upon the character of another person.

We all engage in gossip. Some of us gossip more than others, but the truth is we have all delighted in gossip at one time or another. It brings us a certain adolescent gladness to be in the know. Our egos are inflated and our pride elevated when we are able to tell someone something we know that they don't know, but want to know.

Gossip may begin with facts, but usually is carried away very quickly by speculation into the realm of imagination. Through our speculations—or, even worse, our deceit—we can effortlessly cause enormous harm to other people.

Gossipmongers are cowards and are never true friends. A true friend is interested in helping other people become the-best-versions-of-themselves, but gossip doesn't help anyone become a-better-version-of-himself. Far from it; gossip reduces the character of those who spread it, damages the character of those who listen to it, and often does irreparable damage to the reputation of the person being gossiped about.

Never speak in such a way as to induce your listener to think less of any person. Only open your mouth when it will help people to think better of others. Speak only when your words will help someone become the-best-version-of-themselves. Otherwise remain silent and recollected.

Each of these four maxims requires enormous restraint and discipline. But if you allow them to guide your speech and social interactions, all men and women of goodwill will hold you in the highest esteem.

Nobody likes being talked about behind her back. This is universally true, and yet we are all exposed to situations every day where people are speaking disparagingly about others. If we are to maintain our dignity and defend our integrity, we must learn to handle these social situations with grace and poise. Conversations that have deteriorated into gossip will not naturally return to more elevated subjects. Like water, conversations will run downhill unless we make conscious effort to see that they move in the direction of everyone's best interest (that is, in the direction of our essential purpose).

If someone was being beaten up, I hope you wouldn't stand by and just watch. Perhaps if you were small and weak in comparison to the attacker, you would not be able to physically do anything. But you would at least feel outraged and be able to call for help. Yet every day we stand by while people beat up on people verbally. We stand by and do nothing; perhaps worse still, we don't even feel outraged.

All that is necessary for gossip to triumph is for good men and women to say nothing.

Consider the following ways of defusing a situation of gossip-mongering.

Our first attempt to move a conversation away from gossip may be simply to say, "Perhaps we don't have all the facts." If that doesn't shift the conversation in a more positive direction, you may try saying, "Perhaps we should discuss this next time we are with Mike so that he has an opportunity to tell us what actually happened." And if this does not work, you may say, "I have done many things in my life that I wish I had not; perhaps Mike just had a weak moment," or "Maybe we should give him the benefit of the doubt; I know that if it was me, I sure would like to be given the benefit of the doubt." If all these attempts fail and you know the subject of the gossip, it always helps to remind people, "I will never forget how Mike picked my kids up from practice every week for months, and took them to dinner, when my wife was sick. I will always be grateful to him for that."

Consider how a small fire can set a forest ablaze. The tongue is also a fire. It is so easy to injure a person's reputation in a way that he or she may never be able to recover from. I have been the subject of much gossip and many rumors, some of them malicious. Gossip can hurt us in a way that is impossible to describe; it causes people who may never have met us to judge us and it robs us of an opportunity to make a first impression, because people have had their first impression formed by the gossip they were exposed to.

How do you feel when people speak about you behind your back?

Overcoming gossip in our lives is no easy feat. It can be quite surprising to realize how often we speak about others or partake in a conversation where other people are gossiping. We are then faced with the challenge of learning the social art of avoiding occasions of gossip. And gossip is surprisingly difficult to avoid even when you are making a concerted effort to do so.

Perhaps the great spiritual leaders of the past can help us with this predicament. One of the great spiritual disciplines, which exists in almost all the major traditional and nontraditional religions and spiritualities, is fasting. Fasting is usually associated with food and is performed to free us from cravings and from slavery to the body. Fasting brings clarity to the mind and spirit and allows us to see more clearly who we are and who we are capable of being.

In the previous section we discussed fasting from judgment, and prior to that we discussed fasting from complaining, although we did not discuss them in these terms. Fasting is a traditional spiritual practice usually relating to food, but in essence it can be applied to anything. Perhaps you would like to try this exercise: For the next week, fast from speaking about other people. Fast from gossip. Don't listen to gossip, don't create gossip, and in the coming weeks, months, and years, develop a reputation that gossip is unacceptable in your company.

Some things we fast from temporarily. Other things we fast from in order to form a better habit in our lives. In the case of judgment and gossip, it would be our hope never to return to these destructive ways of thinking and speaking.

If everything should be embraced or rejected according to how it impacts our essential purpose and the purpose of the people around us, then before we ever open our mouths we should ask ourselves: Is what I am about to say going to help anyone become the-best-version-of-himself or herself?

Those of us who are serious about becoming the-best-version-of-ourselves don't have time for gossip. It is the fruit of idleness, and at best a waste of time.

UNDERPAID AND UNDERAPPRECIATED

People almost universally believe that they are underpaid and underappreciated. One of the most powerful ways to use our gift of speech is to offer honest words of appreciation to the people we love, and to the people who help us in large and small ways as we journey through life.

Who doesn't like feeling appreciated? Appreciation seems to make all our hard work and effort seem worth it. Appreciation gives people wings to fly. Nothing encourages and empowers people to go the extra mile like appreciation.

In part one of this book, we discussed the powerful impact appreciation can have on you personally and on the way you see the world and your life. Now let us reflect further on the powerful impact appreciation can have on other people.

In your personal relationships, appreciation is just one way of letting people know that you are grateful for all the ways they enrich your life, and that you care. After all, when you do things for others and they don't in any way express their appreciation, you conclude from their inaction that they are ungrateful and that they don't care.

Let's explore some simple everyday examples.

"Thanks for doing the ironing; there's nothing like putting on one of your freshly ironed shirts."

"I really appreciated you taking the children to school this morning; that extra twenty minutes was just what I needed to get organized for the day."

"Thanks for taking me out for dinner tonight. I had a rough day and I really didn't feel like cooking."

"I love it when you call me in the middle of the day, just to see how my day is going."

"Thanks for listening tonight, I needed to talk through that stuff."

"I was thinking today, I'd be lost without you, and I am so grateful for all the ways you look out for me."

"Thank you for not saying anything this afternoon. I know you had warned me about that and I really appreciate that you bit your tongue and didn't say, 'I told you so,' when you had every reason to."

"I really appreciated the way you gently challenged me to work out today even though I didn't feel like it. I felt so much better about myself when I was done working out."

The spoken word is powerful, and so is the written word. Sometimes our written appreciation can have an enormous impact on the people we love. Did you ever write your parents a letter telling them how much you appreciated all they have done for you? When was the last time you wrote your spouse a love letter?

At every moment a relationship is being driven by positive energy or negative energy. Expressing our appreciation is one way we can inject a very positive energy into our relationships.

The same truth also has powerful applications in the workplace, where appreciation is more valuable than gold, especially if you are managing other people. It stands to reason that employees who feel appreciated are going to be more dedicated to their work than employees who don't feel appreciated. "Underpaid and underappreciated" is a common cry in the workplace, and while we may have little control over the pay scale, appreciation is free.

Even if you are a manager, you probably only have one opportunity a year to give your employees a raise. In many cases, when you do give people a raise, they think you are only compensating them for underpaying them up to that point. On the other hand, you can express your appreciation often. And numerous studies show that there is now a trend away from financial compensation as the main driver in career and job selection. More and more, people are looking for situations where they feel they are making a contribution, situations where they feel their input will be appreciated. In many cases, people are willing to take home a smaller paycheck in exchange. So, as I was saying, appreciation is more valuable than gold—literally. I am not, of course, suggesting that we pay people less because we appreciate them. But in a corporate climate where one of the great challenges is to attract and keep great people, we should not overlook the charismatic power of appreciation. Similarly, as we seek to attract and retain customers, beyond a good product or service nothing is more powerful than convincing customers that they are genuinely appreciated.

Use the power of speech to speak honest words of appreciation at home, at work, and wherever life takes you, and you will be loved more than a giver of gifts. The power of the spoken word is extraordinary when it is used to lavish appreciation upon people. Few things cause the human spirit to soar like genuine appreciation. Appreciation causes people to glow, children and adults alike. Make someone glow today!

USE YOUR WORDS POWERFULLY

If I know nothing else, I know the power of speech. It has the ability to rouse the human spirit, or to defeat it. Speech can inspire the best in people, or discourage them beyond recovery. As children we yearn for the attention and approval of our parents; we want to hear that they are proud of us, that we have pleased them. From time to time, we hear of people whose parents never told them that they love them and we learn how devastating this can be to emotional development.

The use of speech ranges between extremes, with some people unwilling to express their feelings and others unwilling to restrain their tongues in any way at any time. People often apologize for others by saying, "I'm sorry, he has no filter between his brain and his mouth." What could be more absurd? We are not born with that filter; we must discipline ourselves to use our speech for the betterment of our listeners.

The tongue is like money, a terrible master but an excellent servant. The discipline to govern our tongues is important in our quest to become the-best-version-of-ourselves. It is particularly important in our quest to help others achieve their essential purpose. Discipline is the way to becoming the-best-version-of-yourself, and the more we discipline the various aspects of our lives the happier we will be. This discipline is contagious in a very positive manner, as it has a way of spreading from one aspect of our lives to another and from our lives to the lives of those we love. Just transforming the way you speak is discipline enough to bring every other area of your life into focus.

The power of the spoken word can be used in our relationships for better or for worse. How are you using it? I suspect we could all stand to speak a little less about the things that matter least, and a little more about the things that matter most.

ESCAPING THE PRISON OF LONELINESS

When it comes to relationships and intimacy, the things that matter most are those that reveal something about you. Intimacy is gained through the process of self-revelation. The first two levels of intimacy (facts and clichés) are important and useful, but only if they are the precursors of something greater and deeper.

The first two levels of intimacy are very lonely places. If we are unwilling to move beyond clichés and then facts, we build for ourselves a prison of loneliness. There may be plenty of people around, but inside we feel desperately lonely. Whether we are willing to admit it or not, in the first two levels of intimacy we are plagued by a desperate yearning to know and be known, to love and be loved.

We escape this prison of loneliness and move from the second to the third level of intimacy by moving the focus of our conversations from impersonal facts to personal facts. This is the bridge that leads to the third level of intimacy and beyond, but you have to be willing to move past discussions of the weather, sports, and the stock market, to reveal something of yourself.

If you are unwilling to tell me something about who you are and what moves and motivates you, then, quite frankly, you cannot tell me anything I can't read in a book. You become boring and uninteresting, not because you *are* boring and uninteresting, but because you refuse to reveal yourself. If you are willing to reveal yourself, then you've got my attention. If you are willing to share something about you, I'm all ears, because that is something I cannot learn from a book. It is people and personalities that elevate facts and make conversations dynamic and interesting.

The second level of intimacy can be used to develop intimacy or destroy it. The choice is yours. The impersonal facts that are abundant in our lives are supposed to be a warm-up for deeper levels of intimacy. The impersonal facts should lead us to discuss how those facts affect us in deeply personal ways. The impersonal facts should lead us to reflect on our opinions, our hopes and dreams, our feelings, our faults, fears, and failures, and our real and legitimate needs. But too often we use these impersonal facts to block the possibility of intimacy.

The most devastating form of loneliness is not to be without friends; rather, it is to be surrounded by friends and never to be truly known.

Let's face it, nobody ever became truly intimate with another person by discussing the weather, sports, or the stock market. Some may argue that these discussions were the beginning of a great intimacy, and that is quite possible, but let's keep in mind that intimacy is the process of mutual self-revelation. We yearn to know and be known. Unlike the first level of intimacy the second level has the potential to reveal a great deal about a person, but our tendency is to focus predominantly on nonpersonal facts in this second level. Facts are easy and, like clichés, are perceived as safe, especially if they are of the impersonal variety.

But facts can be as trivial and superficial as a discussion of the weather, or as deep and self-revelatory as a discussion of one's childhood. The second level of intimacy can be the beginning of extraordinary communication between two people, or it can be used as a substitute for communication when one or both parties have lost interest in the relationship. Facts can be personal or impersonal. Once again, the choice is ours.

We perceive the first and second levels of intimacy as safe; because we fear true intimacy. The level of clichés and the level of facts are considered very safe because they deal with objective facts and meaningless clichés. We think they are safe because they reveal nothing about ourselves. But there is no reward without risk, and the safety of the first two levels of intimacy depends on their being shallow and superficial. In using them to avoid real intimacy, we lock ourselves in the prison of loneliness. In this self-created prison of loneliness we grow increasingly frustrated, for we never cease to yearn for the one thing we have chosen to avoid: intimacy.

Are you sharing facts in order to further reveal yourself, or are you hiding behind the facts, sharing them in order to avoid sharing yourself?

Sometime in the next twenty-four hours, take a few minutes for this exercise with your significant other. If you don't have a significant other, or if he or she is unwilling to participate, you may choose a friend. Pull two chairs very close to each other and sit so that your knees are touching your partner's. Look into each other's eyes, hold hands, and for three minutes each, take turns telling the other person as many *personal* facts about yourself as come to mind. Try not to lose your eye contact at any time during the three minutes, even if you cannot think of any more personal facts to share.

You will find this a powerful exercise, and it will prepare you well to discover the third level of intimacy. You may wish to repeat it this exercise in relation to each of the remaining five levels of intimacy.

As you sit knee to knee, holding hands, looking into each other's eyes, it is amazing how powerfully the bonds of intimacy can be formed.

CHAPTER NINE

⚬

OPINIONS: THE THIRD LEVEL OF INTIMACY

THE FIRST MAJOR OBSTACLE

Opinions are the first major obstacle we encounter in our quest for intimacy. The realms of cliché and fact tend to be noncontroversial. They don't require us to make ourselves vulnerable, as they do not require any significant self-revelation. The third level of intimacy is the level of opinion. Opinions tend to differ and as a result can often lead to controversy. This is where most relationships begin to find themselves in trouble. The third level of intimacy is the Pandora's box in the process. If we don't learn to master our experience of it, the third level will become the graveyard where we bury many of our relationships.

Most relationships put one foot into the waters of opinions and then jump straight back into facts and clichés. We witness this in conversations all the time. A group of people will be sitting around discussing a particular issue when someone expresses an opinion that someone else (or perhaps everyone else) disagrees with, is uncomfortable with, or is offended by. One of two scenarios usually follows.

Either an argument will break out, or someone will defuse the situation by employing some "surfacing technique." These include changing the subject, making a joke, using sarcasm, and offering a practical diversion, such as asking whether anyone wants some more coffee. These techniques cause the conversation to shoot to the surface like a resurfacing submarine. We all have our favorite surfacing techniques, and we use them to get back to the cliché and fact levels where we generally feel more comfortable and less vulnerable.

Surfacing takes place in conversations and it also happens to entire relationships. If we employ surfacing techniques often enough, over time we train the people around us not to discuss certain topics. If every time someone brings up a certain subject we employ a surfacing technique, we eventually condition her or him not to go there. We use these techniques to mark our boundaries in order to avoid talking about things that make us uncomfortable. By constantly retreating to safe ground, we stay in the shallow and superficial levels of intimacy, we cut off the emotional oxygen, and our relationships begin to atrophy and die.

We want to experience the depths of intimacy. We need to experience the joy of intimacy. But we are afraid.

Like surfacing, arguing results from lack of self-awareness and maturity.

Arguing is the intellectual equivalent of having a temper tantrum, a behavior that most children outgrow by the age of four. By all means have healthy discussions, even lively debates. But arguing tends to become an emotionally charged exchange that disregards the matter at hand and quickly deteriorates into a personal attack. Surfacing moves away from the matter at hand in a more passive way, but can be equally damaging. Both arguing and surfacing distract us from the lively discussion and healthy debate that should be a part of all great relationships.

Learning to be at peace in the company of people who hold and express opinions that completely oppose your own is a sign of great wisdom and extraordinary self-awareness. Most people are simply not able to participate in a discussion without feeling that they have to convince the other person of their opinion. Are we so unsure of our own opinions that we feel threatened by people who express opposing views?

If history has taught us anything, it has taught, time and again, that people will resist with all their strength any attempt you make to impose your opinion upon them. This lesson is demonstrated every day by teenagers in every culture, as it has been demonstrated numerous times throughout history by entire peoples.

Each of us must arrive at our own opinions. We arrive at them through education, experience, and the gentle voice of reason, but never by imposition.

The Importance of a Common Goal

It is here, in the third level of intimacy, that we come face to face with the practical importance of a common goal and purpose. If our essential purpose is to become the-best-version-of-ourselves, and if two people can mutually agree upon the pursuit of this purpose, a great many arguments and disagreements will be avoided.

Our essential purpose brings not only clarity to our lives but also a point of reference to all of our conversations. All opinions can be considered in the light of the overall goal and objective of our lives and relationships.

It is for this reason that couples who can mutually agree to make this essential purpose the goal of their relationship find themselves at a distinct advantage. This common goal provides a reference point. It becomes a point of sanity in many ways.

Most discussions that turn to disagreements that turn to arguments do so because of the failure to find common ground. Once an argument is in process, few people are able to stick to the topic; before you know it, the disagreement is going around in circles or from one point to another. Nobody is listening to anybody else, and most of the participants are more preoccupied with having their say than they are with finding common ground or coming to an agreement. More often than not, when the argument is over nobody knows what it was actually about, because it has taken so many twists and turns along the way.

But when two people (whether it is husband and wife, boyfriend and girlfriend, parent and child, or employee and employer) can agree to place their essential purpose at the center of their relationship as their common goal, all disputes can be discussed in relation to that essential purpose.

If the disagreement is over something as simple as whether to eat takeout or soup and salad for dinner, the common goal offers a reference point for the discussion. And if the disagreement is over something as complex as whether to move your family to a new city a thousand miles from your roots, the common goal still offers a reference point. The reality, however, is that very few relationships have this shared goal, and so many disagreements escalate rapidly into arguments and then quickly degenerate into a battle between egos. Few arguments are ever resolved once they become a battle between egos. These usually result in a standoff, at best.

This is what we see dominating the third level of the great majority of relationships. Most people spend most of their time, effort, and energy in relationships trying to convince each other of their point of view, trying to impose their opinions on each other. In many cases, the conflict is not simply a clash of opinions, but rather a much more significant clash of personal goals and world-views.

If your goal in life is simply to have as much pleasure as you can, and my goal in life is to become the-best-version-of-myself, we are going to disagree at almost every turn. Your personal goal and worldview is one of instant gratification, while mine implies delayed gratification. (But, while we are discussing delayed gratification, let me make it abundantly clear that in no way does this mean that I'm opposed to pleasure. Nor does it mean that I enjoy pleasure any less than the next person, or that it is easier for me to discipline myself than for anyone else. It simply means that I am willing, when my overall goal and purpose require it, to delay pleasure for what I perceive as a greater good.) But because our philosophies and perceived purposes greatly differ, we are going to disagree on just about everything.

This is why a commonly agree-upon purpose is essential to any great relationship. Without it, most relationships meet one of two fates: either they drop back to the superficial forms of communication (facts and clichés), or they become the stage for an ongoing and never-ending battle between two egos.

If you are in a relationship that is under the spell of the latter, the only way to resurrect it is to call a truce in the hope that both of you will recognize that the relationship is not working, and use the cease-fire as an opportunity to agree that from now on you will help each other to become the-best-versions-of-yourselves. If this is not possible, then you are more than likely to become one of those stereotypical couples who have been arguing about the same things, for months, years, decades, perhaps for the whole fifty years of their marriage. Nobody likes being around a couple like that, and nobody likes being part of such a relationship.

What's the problem? The problem is that without an understanding of their meaning and purpose, most relationships quickly become little more than vehicles for the pursuit of selfish and individual goals. Disagreements then become a battle between conflicting interests, rather than a search for a mutually satisfying resolution.

Once the issue is individual gratification rather than collective fulfillment, all arguments become a matter of cunning, pride, and manipulation. This pride and selfishness are the death knell for any relationship. There is no intimacy here, just two people using each other for personal gratification. The result is unavoidably disastrous unless the very motive of the relationship can be changed, from the individual pursuit of gratification to the mutual pursuit of a commonly agreed-upon goal.

In our primary relationships, we must arrive at an agreement that the purpose of the relationship is to help each other become the-best-versions-of-yourselves. This common purpose will provide a touchstone of sanity in every situation and become the great guiding North Star of your relationship. I think you will find that more than 90 percent of disagreements can be settled simply by referring to and invoking the wisdom of the commonly agreed-upon goal and purpose of your relationship.

But even if you are able to place this common purpose at the center of your primary relationship, a great many people will cross your path who do not share your goal and purpose and may even set themselves against it. It is for this reason that we each must learn the arts of agreeing and disagreeing.

LEARNING HOW TO AGREE AND DISAGREE

Knowing how, when, and why to agree or disagree can be a significantly more complex matter than it may at first seem. For some people, agreeing is a way of life; for others, disagreeing is a way of life, as if they have chosen one or the other as a default position. But if relationships are to play the role they are intended to, and help us to change and grow, then it is important to learn to agree and disagree in ways that are healthy.

Great minds and great souls seek out points of genuine agreement with people, but will not agree merely to placate someone. To reach an authentic agreement is often quite difficult, because the agreement must be *genuine*. A genuine agreement is reached when both parties can see the truth of the prevailing point of view. If people are in complete agreement, there is not much of a conversation to be had; on the other hand, the highly argumentative person, who makes a point of disagreeing with everything, can be overwhelming, intensely irritating, and quite tiresome. As with most things in this life, the optimum lies somewhere in the middle.

Agreeing with people is easy if you are willing to set all of your own personal preferences and ideas aside, but nothing is gained through such agreement. There is an art to finding and fostering genuine agreement between people, and it requires a number of disciplines that may seem counterintuitive at first.

In every discussion, we should first seek out what we can agree with in what the other person is saying. Our tendency is to race straight to our point of disagreement.

In every discussion, we should keep in the forefront of our minds that the goal of an authentic discussion is to explore the subject, not to be right. You are not a criminal lawyer who is required to argue the case and attempt to win regardless of the guilt or innocence of the client. In fact, the more each person can remove his or her ego from the discussion and focus on the subject matter, the more fruitful the conversation will be for all involved.

Always make a real effort to see the other person's point of view. Explore the path that has brought the other person to his or her opinion. Try to understand the logic behind that opinion.

Ask yourself whether there are any circumstances in which the other person might be right. If you discover that there are, describe these circumstances and express your agreement with his or her ideas under those circumstances.

Great minds always take genuine delight when points of agreement are discovered, even when the disagreement prevails overall.

Always be open to new ideas and never shut yourself off from the possibility that you may have been wrong.

A mind open to new ideas and willing to engage in dynamic exploration of different subjects is a thing of beauty. A closed mind that is rigidly attached to previously held views and unwilling to entertain new ideas is boring and repulsive.

The art of agreeing is a social and academic grace that few people possess today. Too often, people argue in a vain attempt to assert their authority or superiority. But although the art of agreeing is important, so, too, is the art of disagreeing gracefully if we are to be true to ourselves.

There are people who disagree in a rude and aggressive way. There are other people who disagree for the sport of it, to do battle and to show that they are winning. Some disagree simply to boost their egos. Then there are people who disagree by bullying others. There are people who disagree for no other reason than to showcase their academic superiority, and there are those who disagree because they were raised to believe that is what a conversation is all about. And then there are those who disagree because they know no other way to explore a subject.

It is often tempting to take the path of least resistance and simply agree with people, but learning to disagree in a way that maintains everyone's dignity is critically important in relationships.

When we disagree, we should always do so politely and gently. Aggressive disagreement is no more persuasive, powerful, or valid than gentle disagreement, and often your position will be lost in the emotions created by your aggression.

Any conversation should be a sincere attempt to explore the subject at hand, not a battle between egos. Agreeing and disagreeing are a part of every conversation and every relationship. Learning to do both gracefully requires patience and humility, uncommon virtues in an age obsessed with instant gratification and self-aggrandizement.

UNDERSTANDING VERSUS ACCEPTANCE

In the third level of intimacy, it is impossible to avoid self-revelation. Every opinion says something about who we are. Our opinions also indirectly reveal our core values, expectations, and beliefs. Most people never learn to thrive in the third level of intimacy, because they never develop the maturity necessary to be with people whose opinions differ from their own. Their relationships become boring and begin to slowly die because the waters of the first and second levels cannot satisfy the human heart's thirst for intimacy.

Acceptance is the key to the third level of intimacy. If two people can develop the acceptance necessary to respect each other's opinions, enjoy each other's company despite differences of opinion, and remain dedicated to a common search for truth, then something wonderful happens: the gates of intimacy swing wide open.

Another of the monumental myths propagated by our modern culture is that understanding is the key to having a great relationship. This myth affects the way we treat ourselves and the way we approach everybody who crosses our path. We spend endless amounts of emotional energy trying to figure ourselves out, and equal amounts of energy trying to figure other people out. Consciously or subconsciously, we tell ourselves. "When I understand him, I will accept him" or "When I understand her, I will love her."

This is akin to standing at a stove and saying, "I'll give you wood when you give me heat."

Too often we make understanding a condition of our acceptance. We take the following position: "I don't understand you, therefore I don't accept you and I don't love you." As a result, everyone is held at arm's length. If we are to nurture genuine intimacy, the approach that is needed is radically more proactive and positive: "I love you and I accept you, even though I don't understand you."

It may also be a momentous advance in self-knowledge to examine and note which approach we use with ourselves. Are you able to say, "I love myself and accept myself, even though I don't understand myself"? Or do you hold back acceptance of self, saying, "I don't understand myself, therefore I don't love and accept myself"? The more we are able to accept ourselves, the more we will be able to accept others. Acceptance of others is impossible if we are not able to accept ourselves.

The secret to mastering the third level of intimacy is acceptance. We all thrive when we feel accepted. In the absence of acceptance, we erect all types of barriers and defense systems. These barriers and defenses come down only when we sense that we are safe from judgment and criticism. The essence of relationship is self-revelation, but we will not reveal ourselves if we are afraid of judgment and criticism. Acceptance gives us the courage to be ourselves and freely reveal ourselves. Nothing nurtures relationship like acceptance.

I grew up in a very male-dominated world. I have seven brothers and no sisters, and I attended all-male schools for most of my education. In the absence of much female influence or experience, my mother tried her best to educate us in the ways and needs of women. One thing she said to me when I was a child has never left me: "Women are not to be understood; they are to be accepted." I have grown to believe that this is true not only of women, but of us all. One thing is certain, until we accept people for who they are—male or female—we will never reach the level of intimacy necessary to begin to understand them. We think that when we understand them we will accept them, but it is impossible to understand a person until you accept a person.

When two people develop the maturity to accept each other for who they are and where they are in their own journey, then, and only then, do they really begin to make progress in the quest for intimacy. In any relationship—with your spouse, your teenage child, or your boyfriend or girlfriend—the role and power of acceptance cannot be understated. How many teenagers utter little more than monosyllabic answers to their parents for weeks on end because they sense that whatever they do or say will be judged or criticized? Nonacceptance has them in an emotional fetal position. When we sense nonacceptance, we instinctively respond by withdrawing.

We place too much emphasis on understanding in our relationships, and overlook the extraordinary power of acceptance. What is this acceptance? It is simply allowing people to be themselves, rather than trying to push and cajole them into being who you want them to be or imagine them to be. Acceptance means being a benevolent witness to a person's journey, rather than an emotionally manipulative or dictatorial force in it.

Most of the stress in our lives and in our relationships is caused by our failure to employ acceptance. Have you ever been in a situation where somebody around you was frustrated, restless, angry, and anxious over a situation he had absolutely no control over?

Perhaps an accident had caused a traffic jam. All the traffic was stopped. And this person was carrying on and venting his frustrations. We could see the uselessness of his or her wrestling with the situation. It didn't matter how frustrated, restless, angry, and anxious he became, he couldn't change things. At that moment, the person was actually struggling against the whole universe. We see it clearly in other people, but we don't always see it in ourselves.

I see this type of situation almost every day in airports: a plane is delayed or a flight is canceled because of weather or mechanical difficulties. At the service counter there is a man screaming at the airline agent as if she controls the weather or has an extra hundred-million-dollar aircraft in her garage at home.

We do the very same thing in our relationships. We allow ourselves to become frustrated, restless, angry, and anxious over things that are beyond our control. We wrestle with the moment and in doing so we wrestle with the whole universe. This moment is the culmination of every moment that has preceded it. Stop fighting. Stop resisting. The moment is exactly as it should be. Surrender to it. Immerse yourself in it.

When you become defensive, when you struggle with the moment, your life meets resistance. When you are critical or judgmental, your life meets resistance. When you abdicate responsibility for yourself and your situation, your life meets resistance. When you blame others for your lot in life, you meet resistance. When you refuse to accept the present moment, your life meets resistance.

We must learn to accept and surrender to those moments where we encounter resistance. There is nothing to be gained by forcing the situation. It is an exercise in futility, and, far from diminishing the resistance, will only increase it.

Acceptance is the wisdom to take people, situations, circumstances, and events as they occur, rather than constantly trying to impose our agendas and opinions upon them. Only when we arrive at the wisdom of acceptance do we begin to truly live. Acceptance liberates us. It sets us free to enjoy the moment.

There is a simple prayer of anonymous origins and generally referred to as the Serenity Prayer that has often helped me to celebrate acceptance: "Lord, grant me the serenity to accept the things I cannot change, the strength to change the things I can, and the wisdom to know the difference."

All great things can be achieved only with a light heart. Intimacy is a great thing. It will evade and avoid those who try to control it and those who approach it with heavy hearts, but it will freely give itself to those who approach it with light hearts and gentle spirits. Acceptance gives us that lightheartedness.

While there are many material advantages to living in present times, in some ways modern life places us at a distinct disadvantage in our quest for intimacy. The intellectual demeanor of post-Enlightenment culture fosters a skeptical, sometimes cynical approach that leads us to instinctively question everything. As a result we tend to discount everything that cannot be clearly understood, proven in accepted scientific forms, and explained. While this may be beneficial to our intellectual development, you can see from the preceding discussion of the important role acceptance plays in fostering intimacy how the modern intellectual demeanor leaves us at a distinct disadvantage in our efforts to experience the depths of intimacy.

You cannot understand everything. The universe is full of mysteries. There is hidden meaning behind every event, and each moment is inviting you to become the-best-version-of-yourself. Whatever relationships you find yourself in at this very moment, you have attracted them to your life. You have done so in order to learn from them. If you allow them to, these very relationships, as troubled and turbulent as they may seem, will teach you important lessons and powerfully assist you in your quest to become the-best-version-of-yourself.

Acceptance doesn't mean you have to accept everyone else's opinions and suppress your own. It simply means that you accept other people for who they are and where they are, and recognize that their opinions are the product of their own unique experience of life.

One of the best ways to foster acceptance in your heart, mind, and relationships is to remain open to new ideas. Great minds and souls never completely close themselves off to the possibility that they may be wrong, even when it concerns the ideas, beliefs, opinions, and values they hold dearest. Conversely, mediocre minds and souls tend to be rigidly attached to their ideas and opinions; as a result, very rarely do they change or grow. This closed-minded rigidity is one of the significant impediments that prevent them from ever reaching their full potential. For an honest dialogue to take place, both parties must be willing to entertain the idea that their previously formed ideas, beliefs, and opinions may be wrong. Very few people are secure enough in themselves and their opinions to do this. It is our uncertainty and insecurity that cause us to hold so tightly and narrow-mindedly to our opinions—not our certainty, as we would so often have others believe.

Try always to remain open to new ideas. If you do, I think you will find it much easier to accept people and the great variety of their opinions. One way to foster this acceptance is to develop an understanding of what forms such a variety of opinions in different people.

WHAT INFLUENCES AND FORMS OUR OPINIONS?

Opinions are the most common cause of conflict within relationships, because they give rise to the expectations, beliefs, and the core values that direct our lives. Learning to resolve the conflicts that arise from differing opinions is just one part of nurturing a dynamic relationship. Learning to agree and disagree gracefully is an important component of the conflict resolution process, but it is also important to understand what causes different people to hold different opinions. Why do some good and honest people so fervently hold one view, while other good and honest people with equal fervor oppose it?

Our opinions are largely influenced and formed by experience, education, and friendship. The places we go, the books we read, the schools we attend, and the people we surround ourselves with all have a tremendous influence upon our opinions.

The first realization in our effort to thrive in the third level of intimacy should be that opinions are not static and permanent. Opinions come and go; they are forever changing. The opinions I hold today on a whole variety of issues are dramatically different from what they were ten years ago, and my opinions of ten years ago are vastly different from those I held as a teenager. My opinions are constantly changing, growing, evolving, and being refined.

Once we realize that the opinions we have today are not the same as the opinions we had ten years ago, we realize that the same is true of the people we love, and with that insight we are set free to accept other people and their differing opinions. That opinions are not permanent is an important truth, which we often overlook.

Your opinions are being refined and changing every day, and so are the opinions of your children, parents, friends, colleagues, and significant other. As we become increasingly aware that our own opinions are constantly evolving, we become increasingly tolerant of other people's differing opinions. We are all works in progress. We are all at different points in the journey, and while someone may have a certain opinion today, it doesn't mean that they will always hold that opinion. But if we back him into a corner, aggressively argue with him, let the conversation deteriorate into a personal battle, and make the dispute a matter of pride, he is likely to respond in a rigid and close-minded manner. By your behavior, you can impede his ongoing journey and close the door on authentic intimacy.

Other people's experience of life up to this moment has led them to hold certain opinions, and future experiences will likely cause them to refine those very same opinions. It is not necessary to fight it out. Certainly you can present your ideas, present your opinions, have a lively discussion about the issue, but you have to realize and trust that the other person is at a different point in her journey. Life is going to give her the experiences she needs to become the-best-version-of-herself. Your role is not to impose your opinions.

Think about how your opinions have changed over the past five, ten, fifteen, twenty years? When you were a child, did your parents do and say things that you disagreed with? Do you find yourself saying and doing the same things now with your own children?

Some experiences produce opinions that are biased and prejudiced. For example, I had a wonderful childhood. I was loved, supported, and encouraged, so I grew up believing that the world was a safe and wonderful place full of great people and extraordinary opportunities. Many people have troubled childhoods, during which they are surrounded by people who don't love them or each other. They often grow up believing that the world is a cruel and dangerous place, that nobody can be trusted, and that you have to fight constantly to survive.

Our different experiences give birth to differing worldviews and opinions. New experiences challenge our old perceptions and opinions.

A young man may have grown up under troubled circumstances, like those described above. He may set out upon life's journey believing that the world is a cruel and dangerous place and that nobody can be trusted. But in time he may meet a wonderful young woman and fall in love. Together they may attend college, get married, and raise a family. Through the love of his wife, the expanding vision of ongoing education, and the experience of fathering his own children, he may change his opinions. Ten years later, the same man may tell you that while the world can be a cruel and dangerous place, it can also be a wonderful place filled with extraordinary opportunities; and that, while some people will prove themselves to be unworthy of our trust, others will love us in ways that we never imagined.

Sometimes experience misinforms us and causes us to form opinions and universal assumptions that are erroneous.

Education can just as easily, though often with more seductive charm, create similar biases and prejudices. "There is no such thing as absolute truth. What's true for you may not be true for me" is an idea that is very commonly taught and believed on college campuses across America today. It is the opinion of millions of Americans, but look at the statement closely: "There's no such thing as absolute truth." This is, in itself, a statement that is being made absolutely. That is to say, it applies some rule or standard to everyone without exception.

The other problem is that while this idea (or opinion) gets a lot of airtime, nobody actually believes it. If someone said to you, "There's no absolute truth," and you shot him in the foot, he probably wouldn't be too happy. But by his own creed, he would have to accept that while shooting someone may be wrong for him, it might not be wrong for you. At this, the relativist will most likely amend his original statement by saying, "As long as you are not hurting others, you're free to do and believe whatever you wish." The problem is, this is both an arbitrary distinction and another absolute statement. Who says I can't hurt others? Who decides what constitutes "hurt"? Where does the rule come from?

The argument that there is no absolute truth is often cited when people disagree with a statement and have no other way to support their opinion. It is the classic example of how education can mislead and misinform.

At the same time, education can be a powerful force in the expanding vision of the world and ourselves. Education can be a powerfully instrument in the tearing down of biases and prejudices, thus transforming us into men and women with large hearts and beautiful minds.

Both education and experience are constantly influencing our opinions, and as a result our opinions are constantly being refined. Learning to thrive in the third level and moving beyond it depend upon acceptance. Knowing that opinions are not permanent, but rather dynamic and changing, liberates us to enjoy people for who they are today. Only if we place this type of acceptance at the core of our relationships will we continue to experience deeper levels of intimacy.

THE FIRST TRUTH

The first truth of relationships is that all relationships have problems. They all have unresolvable problems. These unresolvable problems are usually the result of vastly different opinions on certain issues or varying expectations about the role each partner should play. All of these are the result of differences in upbringing, education, and experience.

Too often we subscribe to the fantasy that we are more suited for each other than are other couples, and that therefore our relationship is different and better. The truth is, we all face the same challenges along the way, and most relationships have more similarities than they do differences. If we have the courage to look beyond our illusions, we discover the daunting reality that all relationships have unresolvable problems. And believe it or not, it is how we choose to deal with these unresolvable problems that most influences the quality and depth of our relationships.

The relationships that thrive despite their unresolvable problems are those in which the people acknowledge the problems, find ways to adapt to them, and over time even find them amusing. They don't allow differing opinions to become a roadblock in their quest for intimacy.

The people whose relationships struggle take a very different path when confronted with their unresolvable problems. They constantly argue to the point of gridlock, they keep hurting each other's feelings, and consciously or subconsciously they stand at the stove saying, "I'll give you wood when you give me heat." They withhold their love, affection, and acceptance from each other while promising themselves, "When I understand her I will accept and love her," and vice versa. Over time a pattern emerges. The people disagree about something; they criticize each other; they blame each other for their inability to resolve their differences; the tension escalates; the subject of the argument is abandoned for condescending and critical personal attacks; the argument becomes too painful, so one person (or both) abdicates; they retreat from the conflict and return to the superficial and safer levels. Unless they can learn a new way to deal with their unresolvable problems they will never taste the life-giving waters of intimacy. The new way they desperately need to find is acceptance.

How do you deal with unresolvable problems in your primary relationship? With your children? With your parents? With friends? At work?

We must work our way out from under the illusion that all

problems can be resolved. Once we are liberated from the expectation that we should be able to resolve all the problems in our relationships, we are free to turn our attention to helping each other become the-best-versions-of-ourselves.

It isn't your job to fix the relationship. It is the relationship's job to fix you.

Relationships are hard work, but the hardest work is letting go of our personal agendas and learning to accept that we are who we are and where we are *right now* for a reason. Everything doesn't have to be planned and controlled. Relationships should be treated as sacred mysteries. Allow the mystery to unfold in its own time.

The greatest gift we can give anyone in relationship is acceptance. Once we resolve to accept people for who they are and where they are, we are set free and so are they. We are free to affirm them, encourage them, and appreciate them, and by liberating ourselves we set them free to be who they are and become all they were created to be.

All relationships have unresolvable problems. It is difficult to come to terms with this truth at first, but in time you will discover, if you have not done so already, that it is how we deal with these unresolvable problems that usually determines the fate of our relationships. Very few relationships lose their footing in the midst of great joy or even the everyday challenges; it is the unresolvable problems of relationships (and the illusion that they should not exist) that cause us to lose our footing.

COLLECTIVE EGO

Relationship is about teamwork, not about getting what you want. In fact, relationships are not about *getting* at all. They are about giving and receiving, about working together for the common good and toward the achievement of a common goal. A relationship is about helping someone else become the-best-version-of-himself or herself, and receiving the support you need to become the-best-version-of-yourself. All of this requires a highly developed sense of teamwork.

One of the obstacles we encounter in any form of teamwork is ego. The ultimate dysfunction in a relationship occurs when the individuals within that relationship seek personal fulfillment at the expense of the team.

Relationships are about teamwork. You and your spouse are a team. You and your teenage child are a team. You and your girl-friend or boyfriend are a team. How's your team doing?

For any relationship to be truly dynamic and successful, the collective ego of those involved must be greater than their individual egos. Two must become one. Everything has to be subordinate to the goal and purpose of the team. Individual achievement means nothing if it doesn't help the team achieve its goals. If the team loses, everyone loses.

Most teams fail not because they lack talent but because they lack the character necessary to subjugate personal ambition to a common purpose.

If you want to learn about teamwork, study great teams and study great coaches. I've already mentioned John Wooden, ar-guably the greatest coach in college basketball history. From time to time, he would get a player who didn't really care about results. Or at least, not team results. Such a player was interested only in his own statistics and the individual recognition those statistics could bring him. If the team lost, that didn't bother him, as long as he was getting his points. If the team won and he didn't score enough, he would be unhappy. Coach Wooden would put that kid on the bench week after week after week, because even if he was the most talented player on the court, the team played better without him. Great coaches don't put the best players on the court, they put the best team on the court.

Teams are most successful when the collective ego is greater than the individual egos. No matter how well an individual performs, if the team loses, everyone loses. You may get a promotion and a huge pay raise, but if work causes you to neglect your spouse, your children, your exercise regimen, and your spiritual disciplines, then your team loses.

Intimacy requires teamwork. In the third level of intimacy we come up against the obstacle of differing opinions. Some people run from the conflict and head straight back to the shallow and superficial waters of facts and clichés. Others set up camp here in the third level and continue to do battle over their differing opinions for the rest of their lives. But a rare few learn that opinions are constantly changing and evolving. This gives birth to the wisdom of acceptance, which in turn allows them to find creative ways to live with their unresolvable problems. The fruit of all this is the formation of a team, and with their collective ego to guide and protect them this team is ready to experience the deeper mysteries of intimacy.

CHAPTER TEN

꧁ ꧂

HOPES AND DREAMS: THE FOURTH LEVEL OF INTIMACY

THE VISION THAT SHAPES OUR LIVES

Dreams are a fascinating part of the human experience. Every dream is unique. Our dream world, however confusing, frightening, wonderful, or exhilarating, reveals something about who we are. No emotion is off limits in our dreams. Sometimes our hidden self, the one we try to keep hidden from the world and even from the people we love, emerges in our dreams. Our dreams very often reveal our hopes, fears, fantasies, and our deepest desires.

Dreams have always fascinated man, while the meanings behind them have always evaded us. Who hasn't spent the empty moments of a day wondering, "I wonder what that dream I had last night means?"

A couple of years ago, a friend of mine gave me a dream dictionary for Christmas. This book claims to elucidate the meaning of thousands of dreams. You can look up various words, places, people, and things, and the dream dictionary explains the significance of these things to your dream. I kept the book on my bedside table for several months, and each morning I would look up the meaning of my dreams. It was a fascinating exercise. But the dreams that we have while we sleep are not what the fourth level of intimacy is about. The fourth level of intimacy is about the dreams we have for our lives, our relationships, our future, the brief time we have here on earth.

Hopes and dreams are a crucial part of life and of any healthy relationship. While they are very much focused on and concerned with the future, they also say something real about who we are now. The fourth level of intimacy is about knowing what your hopes and dreams are in each of the many facets of your life; just as important, it is about revealing your dreams to your significant other (and, where appropriate, the other people with whom you share your other high-level relationships).

The reason that it is so important to learn to thrive in the third level of intimacy by accepting each other in spite of our differing opinions is because we generally reveal our dreams only to people we feel accepted by. Our dreams speak significantly about who we are, so they are a point of significant vulnerability. When we are around people who are judgmental and critical, we usually don't make ourselves vulnerable. For this reason, we never experience true intimacy with people who are constantly critical and judgmental.

Before we make ourselves vulnerable, we assess, consciously or subconsciously, whether we are in a supportive environment with people who accept us. Acceptance melts our defenses, removes our masks, and gives us the courage to reveal ourselves. Dreams are an intimate part of who we are, and while we may share some of our shallower and more superficial dreams with many people, there are other dreams so deep and so intimate that at certain times in our lives we are unwilling to admit them even to ourselves.

Intimacy is the mutual self-revelation that causes us to know and be known. Being aware of the dreams of the people you love is just as important as knowing your own dreams. Once we know each other's dreams, we must decide whether we are going to help each other fulfill them. Then, the more important decision usually occurs when you have to decide which dreams have priority. The litmus test remains the same: which of these dreams will help us become the-best-version-of-ourselves? Everything makes sense in relation to our essential purpose, including dreams. Our hopes and dreams are only helpful if they help us to become the-best-version-of-ourselves. The dreams that do should be embraced, pursued, and celebrated. Those that do not should be rejected.

Knowing the dreams of the people you love and helping them fulfill those dreams brings a certain dynamism to relationships that is both energizing and inspiring. Few things energize an individual like the passionate pursuit of a dream, and few things can infuse a relationship with such energy and enthusiasm as the pursuit of dreams. Revealing your dreams, chasing your dreams, and encouraging the people you love to fulfill their dreams can have a very powerful impact on any relationship. The fourth level of intimacy is about learning how to do that in the relationships that are most important to you.

Our dreams are the vision that shapes our lives, and the vision that shapes our relationships.

THE QUESTION OF GRATIFICATION

When it comes to the pursuit of dreams, the first question to ask yourself is, Are you willing to delay gratification? If your answer to this question is no, then relationships are no place for you, and any worthwhile dream will evade you. The present culture proposes that life is about getting what you want, when you want it. This culture is propelled forward by a constant need for gratification and a contempt and disdain for anything that would delay our gratification. We no longer live in a culture of instant gratification. We now live in a culture where instant gratification isn't fast enough. As a result, we are now witnessing the rise of entire generations who possess no patience, little self-control, and an almost complete inability to discipline themselves.

The reality is that success in any field, whether it is business, career, sports, investing, health and well-being, spirituality, or relationships, requires delayed gratification. More, our success in any realm of life depends on delayed gratification. You cannot be successful without delaying gratification—unless your goal is instant gratification. And if this is your goal, you may experience some temporary success but you are doomed to fail sooner or later.

Consider Michael Jordan and Lance Armstrong, two of the most extraordinary athletes of our age, and arguably of all times. They have lived lives of extraordinary achievement and phenomenal success, but behind every achievement and success we find an uncommon ability to delay gratification. Why don't we want to delay gratification? The reason is that doing so is painful to a greater or lesser extent. The pain may not be physical, but pain comes in many forms, as anyone who has experienced the loss of a loved one is well aware.

Sometimes the pain amounts simply to less pleasure. For example, you feel like a hamburger and fries. Why? They represent a momentary pleasure to you. Instead, you have soup and a salad. You still have the pleasure of eating, though perhaps less pleasure than you might have had from the burger and fries. You choose to delay the gratification. If you don't eat the burger and fries, isn't the gratification lost forever? No, you just can't get your mind off the burger and fries. So, what is the gratification that you have delayed? The future gratification is looking and feeling healthier.

We associate delayed gratification with pain, and we should. But we also consider pain to be bad, and that is a mistake. One of the great differences between Michael Jordan and Lance Armstrong and their competitors is that Jordan and Armstrong are able to endure more pain. Why? They have practiced enduring more pain. Men and women of towering success befriend pain in one form or another. While the mediocre masses wander through history avoiding pain whenever possible, the heroes, leaders, legends, champions, and saints of every age befriend pain. You think of pain as an enemy; they think of it as a friend.

On the morning of game five of the NBA finals between the Chicago Bulls and the Utah Jazz, in June 1997, Michael Jordan woke up violently ill. Nobody was sure whether it was food poisoning or altitude sickness, but at eight A.M. Jordan's bodyguards called Chip Schaefer, the team trainer, to tell him that Jordan was deathly ill. It was later reported that Jordan had woken with a fever of 103: that was not true. His temperature was *only* 100. When Schaefer arrived at Jordan's room, he found the megastar pathetically weak, in fetal position, and wrapped in blankets. He had not slept at all the night before, had a blinding headache, and had suffered violent nausea throughout the night. He may have been the greatest player in the world, but there was no way he would be playing any basketball that day. Or was there?

Schaefer hooked Jordan up to an IV to get as much fluid into him as possible and gave him some medication to help him rest for the morning. He had worked closely with Michael Jordan, and understood more than most the inexplicable drive that possessed him. Jordan had an invincible spirit that allowed him to push on long after most people's bodies would have betrayed them. Schaefer had seen this spirit in 1991, during the finals against the Lakers. Jordan had badly injured his toe and Schaefer had worked tirelessly to create a shoe that would protect Jordan's injury during the next game. But when Jordan tried the shoe before the game he discovered while it eased the pain, it hindered his ability to start, stop, and cut. "Give me the pain," he said to Schaefer.

The story behind the making of the legend we know as Lance Armstrong is frighteningly similar. Armstrong is the seven-time winner of the Tour de France, unquestionably the most grueling human endurance test on two wheels. Every July all of Europe (and, since the emergence of Armstrong, most of the world) turns its attention to France and the bike race that encircles it, covering more than 2,226 miles in twenty-one days. The hundreds of riders who start can all ride a bike, they can all make the distance, but few can endure the pain it takes to win. The tour is an endurance test, and what is it that the competitors have to endure? Pain. One of Armstrong's more famous remarks is "Pain is temporary, but quitting lasts forever."

Our ability to delay gratification determines our success in a great many areas of our lives.

Personal finance is another great example, perhaps one many of us will be able to relate to a little more closely. Millions of Americans retire every year with little or no net worth. Having given the best forty years of their life to work, they have frighteningly little to show for it. They will collect their Social Security, and thanks to the structures and supports of this great nation they will survive, but a great many of them will spend the rest of their lives watching pennies. Is there an alternative?

Absolutely. If you saved $1 a day for 55 years you would have $20,000 in savings. You may say, So what? Well, if you invested your $30 at the end of each month in government bonds at a return of 5 percent, after 55 years you would have $101,000. Still not convinced that you should delay your gratification? Invest your $1 a day at a return of 9 percent, and after fifty-five years you will have $481,795. Is it unreasonable to expect a return of 9 percent? You decide, but the S&P has averaged a return of 12.4 percent since 1925.

Still not convinced? Save an entire $3 a day for fifty-five years and invest it at 9 percent and you will walk away with $1,445,385. That's right, almost one and half million dollars in return for $3 a day of delayed gratification. Increase your savings to $5 a day and you will amass $2,408,975. Why do most people retire with little or no net worth? Two reasons. They are unwilling to delay gratification, and they never really took the time to develop a financial dream.

On the other hand, the average household in the United States that carries a credit card balance has more than $7,000 of credit card debt.

Consumer debt is at record levels. Instant gratification is at record levels. Coincidence? I think not. Is the battle between saving and spending? I don't think so. The battle is between instant gratification and delayed gratification.

I am not suggesting that wealth is the be-all and end-all, but given a choice between riches and poverty I would choose wealth every time. And I'd encourage you to do the same. The reality is that most of us are given the choice between riches and poverty.

Now consider relationships. Think about the people you know who have flailing relationships or who cannot keep a relationship together. Are they willing to delay gratification? Do they see relationships simply as a source of pleasure? Do they hold the unreasonable expectation that a good relationship should not have problems? Are they willing to put the relationship ahead of their personal agendas and pleasures?

Every worthwhile dream demands delayed gratification, and

the dream of a great relationship is no different. Every day another book about relationships is published that tells you how to go out and get what you want. If this is the approach we take to relationships, we are doomed from the very start. The very nature of relationship is giving, not getting; it is helping someone else in their journey. In order to approach a relationship in this way, we must at the very least be willing to set our own desires and agendas aside initially. We must be willing to delay our own personal gratification. Does this mean that we should always suppress our desires? Not at all. Does this mean we should always delay our gratification? Absolutely not. It simply means that there will be times in your relationship when you will be required to delay gratification (individually and as a couple) if you wish to live the dream of a great relationship, and if you wish to achieve some of the other dreams you have as individuals and as a couple within the relationship.

The achievement of our dreams is inseparable from delayed gratification.

The willingness and ability (which is the result of nothing other than practice) to delay gratification is as important to relationships as it is to any other area of life.

So, how do the people who delay their gratification do it? They keep in mind the future gratification. Michael Jordan never let his dream to become the best basketball player in history leave his mind. When training got tough, Lance Armstrong reminded himself of his dream to win a Tour de France, and then another, and another, and then a record-breaking six. Men and women who build wealth keep in mind the opportunities the wealth they are building will give them (and the people they love) in the future. Those who are able to delay their gratification do so by reminding themselves of the reward that their sacrifices will bring. They delay their gratification by keeping their eyes firmly fixed on their dreams. What else do they do? They practice, and they practice, and they practice. They practice delaying gratification, so that gradually they build up immunity to the pain. As their tolerance for pain increases, they are able to push themselves further and further, thus creating even higher levels of success. Finally, they imagine how sweet their future victory (gratification) will be. They live with the dream in mind.

The dream gives them reason and inspiration to delay their gratification. More often than not, people who are unwilling to delay gratification simply don't have a dream worth delaying their gratification in order to achieve. Do you?

Delayed gratification gets us thinking about the future, and in relationships that is critical. When we love someone, we think about building a life with that person and about all the exciting possibilities the future holds. When we are interested only in fulfilling our personal desire for pleasure and in instant gratification, we don't think about the future or even about the other person. We think about now and about no one but ourselves.

Dreams extend our time horizon beyond the self-centeredness of instant gratification and into a future filled with the love, intimacy, and mutual respect for which we all yearn. Dreams, a common purpose, and the willingness to delay gratification will ignite your relationship like no pleasure the world has ever prescribed.

BUILDING A FUTURE TOGETHER

Dreams tell you a lot about a person—not only about who he is today but also about the person he hopes to become in the future. Dreams tell us about what a person values, what he is passionate about, and what he centers his life upon. So if you are deciding if you want to spend your life with a person, knowing what his hopes and dreams are can very often tell you something about the person he will become.

The fourth level of intimacy is about discovering each other's dreams. Knowing what brings passion, energy, and enthusiasm to the lives of the people you love is crucial if you are going to develop a deep level of intimacy.

The reason it is so important to know the dreams of the people we love is that they view their lives in relation to their dreams, and so do you. Our dreams are the lenses through which we view everything. Let me give you an example. Your wife says to you, "I saw a beautiful dress at the store today. I think I'll go back and buy it tomorrow." You may ask how much it costs, to which she replies, "Two hundred and fifty dollars." It is an arbitrary amount and many people could justify the expenditure. But you may become upset because you see this expenditure as frivolous. As you see it, your wife already has fifty dresses that she hardly ever wears. But this is not the point; you are not upset because your wife wants a new dress. The real point is that you would rather see this money used for something else—that is, for one of your dreams.

Your dream may be to retire early and travel with your wife while you are still young enough to enjoy it. You may be saving relentlessly to make this dream come true, but you haven't told your wife about it. You may have alluded to it, but have you sat down together, done the math, and determined what you both need to do to make the dream a reality? Let's face it: if you gave your wife the choice between a handful of new dresses and traveling together after your early retirement, I think she would pick the latter. If she wouldn't, then you've got bigger problems than whether or not she buys the dress.

Dreams bring clarity and focus to our relationships. If you are going to build a future together, you have to know each other's dreams.

In *The Rhythm of Life,* I spoke briefly about my dream book. My dream book is a small journal-like book that I write all my dreams in, everything from places I want to go and things I would like to own, to books I would like to write and virtues I would like to possess. Every day I take time to flip through my dream book, perhaps while I am on a plane, or working out on the treadmill, or just lying in bed before I go to sleep.

Dreams have to be written down, and we have to take time each day to remind ourselves of our dreams. Otherwise we get distracted from what matters most by the things that matter least.

The same is true in our relationships. It is so easy to get carried away by the hustle and bustle of our everyday lives and forget to give our dreams the attention they deserve.

Isn't it time you had a dream book?

Isn't it time you had a dream book as a couple?

Get yourself a journal to use as a dream book. Next time you see that watch, car, or vacation you really want in a magazine, cut the advertisement out and stick it in your dream book. These are the easy ones.

Maybe what you really need is a dream weekend? Not a dream vacation—a weekend away with your significant other to do some serious dreaming.

I look at seven areas of my life when I have my dream sessions: physical, emotional, intellectual, spiritual, professional, financial, and adventurous.

Do some dreaming. Look at each of the seven areas and talk about what your dreams are in each of them. Write down the dreams. You will have individual dreams, and dreams as a couple. But write them down, and then start to set some goals. Goals are dreams with a deadline. Look at each of the seven areas and set some goals with a deadline one year from now.

One of your physical goals might be to lose some weight or to exercise together regularly. I hope one of your emotional goals is to have a great relationship, and in part three I am going to help you define more clearly what that means to you. You may have been wanting to read more books for years; perhaps that will be one of your intellectual goals, or maybe you have always wanted to go back to school. You may be yearning to get away on a retreat to explore your spirituality a little more. This could be your spiritual goal. If you have been complaining that you hate your job, perhaps your professional goal will be to find a new job. Have you been putting off saving? Maybe your financial goal will be to formulate a financial plan and start saving. And in the area of adventure, perhaps you have always wanted to go white-water rafting, or parachuting, or to learn to fly.

The thing about dreams is that the more you define them, the more likely you are to achieve them. Dreams don't just happen to come true. People make dreams come true.

Goals drive us. Goals bring the best out of us. Goals and dreams challenge us to look at the world and ourselves in a different way. Goals flood our lives with passion, purpose, and energy. And goals will do all of this for your relationships also. Stop coasting along; dream, and set some goals that will lead to the fulfillment of those dreams.

As human beings, we are most fully alive when we are changing and growing and stretching our boundaries in our quest to be all we can be. As a result, we respond very well to goals. The art of goal-setting means choosing goals that are challenging but attainable—that is, not so easy that you are not challenged, and not so difficult that you become discouraged. If you have an enormous dream, you may need to break it down into several stages, each defined by its own smaller and more manageable goals.

Take yourselves away on a dream weekend; if you can't get away for the weekend, for whatever reason, block off a couple of evenings, or a Sunday afternoon. And make it a goal to go away for the next dream-making session one year from now.

Come up with a plan. Identify the goals and dreams you want to achieve in the next twelve months. Some dreams take longer than one year to bring to fruition, but define what part of that dream has to be achieved in that first year. Write the plan down. Make two copies. Carry it with you so that when you have a few moments in the middle of your day you can read through it. Perhaps on the last day of each month the two of you could take some time to talk about how you are progressing.

If you have children, encourage them to dream: get them a dream book and take some time as a family to write down your individual dreams and talk about them. There is something powerful about helping the people we love chase and fulfill their dreams.

Too often, we live in the miscredited fantasy that one day we will wake up and everything will be exactly as we have always wished it would be. It won't. You know that, somewhere deep inside of you. And that is the difference between a wish and a dream.

If you truly want to be intimate with the people you love, you need to know what drives them. In different stages of our lives we are driven by different things; that is why it is so important to make this an annual exercise with regular review throughout the year. If you asked your spouse what his or her dreams were when you first starting dating and you haven't spent much time on the subject since, you will likely discover that he or she has a whole new set of dreams now. If this is the case, may I suggest you ask this question of your significant other as a starting point for the renewal in your relationship: Which of your dreams got lost along the way while I was too busy pursuing my own?

CHAPTER ELEVEN

⚭

FEELINGS: THE FIFTH
LEVEL OF INTIMACY

ARE YOU WILLING TO MAKE
YOURSELF VULNERABLE?

The fifth level of intimacy is the level of feelings. Feelings are defined as "emotional reactions" and we have thousands of them every day. A blue sky when you first wake in the morning may cause an emotional reaction: a feeling. A dreary, cloud-filled sky may provoke a very different feeling. What was your last emotional reaction? What are you feeling at this very moment? Some feelings come and go and we pay very little, if any, attention to them. Other feelings have strength that can possess us if we allow them to.

Knowing our feelings and sharing our feelings is an integral part of intimacy. The fifth level is about exploring how we feel about different people, places, things, and events, and learning how to share those feelings in a way that allows the people we love to know us on a deeper level.

At this level of intimacy, we come face to face with the fear of rejection that we discussed in the opening chapter of this book. The facts of our lives say something about who we are. Our opinions say something about how we have responded to the facts of our lives. Our hopes and dreams say something about how we want to live our lives and the persons we are striving to become. Each of these reveals something about us, and to the extent that we reveal ourselves we become vulnerable. Our feelings are the raw emotional nerve endings that very often reveal our brokenness, our humanity, our need to be held, listened to, and loved. The revelation of our feelings makes us extremely vulnerable.

The challenge of the second level of intimacy is, Are you willing to move beyond the cliché and say something about yourself? The challenge of the third level of intimacy is, Are you willing to reveal your opinions and offer the gift of acceptance to those with opinions different from your own? The challenge of the fourth level of intimacy is, Are you willing to set aside instant gratification in order to build a future together?

The challenge of the fifth level of intimacy is, Are you willing to make yourself vulnerable? If you are not willing to let your guard down, take your mask off, make yourself vulnerable, and tell your significant other how you really feel, then you will not have intimacy. At every point in the journey to deeper and deeper levels of intimacy, a price must be paid. The price the fifth level asks of us is that we make ourselves vulnerable.

VULNERABLE BUT THERAPEUTIC

Revealing our feelings makes us vulnerable, but we endure risks in order to reap rewards. The reward of making ourselves vulnerable is mental health. At the heart of all successful psychotherapy is a relationship in which a person can say anything, tell everything, and reveal the very core of his being, just as a little child will tell his mother everything. Isn't this what millions of people go to therapists for every year? Could it be that if we all had just one genuinely intimate relationship, there would be no need for therapists?

How beautiful and liberating it must be to have nothing to hide. When people are willing to reveal themselves to each other in a spirit of honesty, acceptance, and reverence, they liberate each other from the insanity of isolation and loneliness. Who doesn't want a relationship in which they can tell everything?

We all have so much bottled up inside us. It is this emotional coagulation that makes us mad. And it causes disease in ways that, I suspect, we have not even begun to understand. We all sense that we have something to say, but don't know quite how to say it or whom to say it to.

Intimacy is a risk. It should not be taken lightly, but we must take it. No man or woman can live a full life without being known by at least one person. Intimacy is a prerequisite for all those who wish to live the abundant life. The only true reason to delay the adventurous and risky pursuit of real intimacy is the absence of a confidant freely chosen and worthy of our trust.

But we cling to safety and idolize security, all the time overlooking the fact that safety and security are just illusions. You are only safe until you are no longer safe. You are secure only until you are no longer secure, and our illusions are ripped out from under us quickly and without warning. What good are your safety and security if you or a loved one is tragically killed in a accident tomorrow?

If you gave an unborn child the choice between staying in her mother's womb and coming out into this extraordinary world, the child would choose the womb every time. The child knows the womb, and we love what we know. The womb is safe, secure, and warm, and the child thinks she has everything she needs in the womb. Given the choice, and knowing nothing of what is outside the womb, the child would choose the world she knows.

Sometimes when it comes to intimacy, you and I are that unborn child. We don't see the world that awaits us. After all, it is only by truly experiencing intimacy that we come to realize what a great need we have as humans to be really listened to, to be taken seriously, to be accepted, encouraged, and understood. Only those who have experienced the new world of intimacy know how important it is to move beyond the world of self. Unable to comprehend the powerful ways that intimacy can move us, challenge us, energize us, and liberate us, most people cling to the little that they have and convince themselves that they have too much to lose. Too often, too many of us settle for crumbs from the table of the most exquisite banquet of all times, the banquet of intimacy.

If you are unwilling to embrace the challenge of making yourself vulnerable, intimacy will elude you until circumstances or necessity convinces you to change your mind. Intimacy is unattainable for those who refuse to take the risk of making themselves vulnerable in their high-level relationships, and particularly their primary relationship.

HEALTHY EXPRESSION

We all have a legitimate need to express our feelings, but there are a number of factors that contribute to the healthy expression of feelings. As with most things, it may help to ask ourselves: Who? What? When? Where? How? Why?

Who? is perhaps the most important factor, but we should start with Why? because what we hope to achieve determines everything else.

If you just need to say something out loud, almost anyone will do. In fact, if you just need to say something out loud, go into an empty room, close the door, and speak.

If you need to express feelings about a certain person, then that person is probably the best person to hear whatever you have to say. But remember, if your feelings are critical, be sure to express them with the spirit of helping him become the-best-version-of-himself.

But assuming that your feelings are of a more complex and intimate nature, and that what you are really looking for is someone to listen to you and try to understand what you are feeling, then there is a good chance your primary relationship is where this communication belongs.

Expressing your feelings to an infant child is unlikely to produce the response necessary to make you feel that you have been heard and understood. It may be unfair to express your feelings about a serious matter to your adolescent child, who is unlikely to be able to support you in the way you need and who may be prematurely burdened with the worry of a certain situation. The person bagging your groceries probably isn't the right person, and neither is the new neighbor across the street.

The What?, of course, is entirely up to you, though when expressing our feelings we should try to use "I" statements that focus on the facts (or specifics). This is the How? For example, "I am angry because you came home late from work and you missed dinner with the family." In this way, you are expressing the way you feel ("I am angry"), giving the reason and describing the event that provoked that feeling ("because you came home late from work"), and explaining the effect the event had on your relationship ("and you missed dinner with the family"). It is also important to note that even if you are angry, you don't have to choose to express you feelings with anger. If you are hurt, you should try not to express your feelings in a way that is hurtful to another (even to the person who provoked your feeling of hurt).

Timing is everything, they say. There are three times when nobody should ever try to have a conversation with me that requires any level of active focus and deep listening: when I first wake up in the morning; when I first arrive at my office for the day; and when I first arrive home from a trip. I don't need hours; I just need ten minutes to get settled. The people around me have learned to allow me that time before they ask me to address any matter that requires a clear mind and my undivided attention.

We should learn which times are best for intimate conversations with the people we love. Sometimes timing alone can determine whether we have a level one or a level five communication with a person. And so, even when we need to express our feelings, we should avoid reducing that need to another form of instant gratification. Otherwise our expression of our feelings becomes no more elevated than a child's tantrum in a shopping mall, or a teenager shouting expletives because he lacks the vocabulary and maturity to genuinely express his feelings.

One very powerful tool may be to say, "I really need a few minutes to talk some time today." Because the other person elects the time, she will usually be at her most attentive and receptive. All of this assumes that there is mutual respect between you, and that you are both trying to help each other become the-best-version-of-yourselves. Where this common goal cannot be established, the pursuit of intimacy at every level is significantly more difficult.

This leaves us with the Where? My own generation spends so much of its time in environments filled with deafening music that it comes as no surprise to me that many of my peers, even those in long-term relationships, have little intimacy.

If you want to have a conversation that advances the intimacy between you and your significant other, child, parent, or just about anybody, the place to do it is not in front of the television, in a bar where you can hardly hear each other, or in a group. Certain environments encourage intimacy; usually these are quiet places where you can have time with each other and not be interrupted by other people.

Learning to express our feelings in healthy ways takes time. Different people respond in different ways to the What?, When?, Where?, How?, and Why? Part of the process of intimacy is getting to know the most effective times, places, and ways to communicate, so we can optimize our chances of successful and fruitful communication.

BABY STEPS LEAD TO SECOND NATURE

At first, sharing your feelings with each other may be like pulling teeth, but in time this will become a habit and eventually it will become second nature. If we are really attentive to each other, over time we will begin to notice that the people we love are feeling a certain way before they tell us, and sometimes even before they have become consciously aware of it themselves.

When I have something on my mind or am feeling a little stressed, I whistle. It is usually a very light and happy tune, and strangers probably think, "He must be very happy today." The people who know me well know better. I don't remember ever deciding consciously to whistle, and more often then not I don't realize I am doing it until someone who knows me well asks, "What's on your mind?" And that's when I become aware that I was whistling. Similarly, you get to know the people around you, and as you grow in intimacy, you'll become aware of certain signs that reveal how they are feeling.

We can master the different levels of intimacy only by practice, and in the case of the fifth level that means taking time regularly to express our feelings. If I were to say that it was necessary to do this at least once a day, or several times a day, many would cringe, because at first the expression of our feelings can seem so unnatural and uncomfortable. I suspect it is like riding a roller coaster: at first it is frightening, but in time you become comfortable with it and even learn to relax, let go, and enjoy it. (Needless to say, intimacy has some significant advantages over riding roller coasters.) Now, you may never become comfortable expressing feelings of hurt, but you will develop the courage to express them nonetheless. You may never enjoy expressing your anger, but you will develop healthy ways to express it.

In the fifth level of intimacy, we once again come to understand the central importance of the acceptance developed in the third level. Acceptance gives us the courage to make ourselves vulnerable by sharing our feelings. Confident that they will not be judged or criticized but rather accepted for who they are and where they are on our journey, most people will open the doors of their hearts. We keep those doors so tightly closed mainly out of fear of criticism, judgment, and rejection. If you can convince the people you love that you accept them for who they are, that you are not out to change them at every turn, and that you will try to understand them as well as you can, they will respond by revealing themselves, and you will both enjoy the mystery of intimacy.

Over time, as we become more and more comfortable with each other, as we become more and more convinced of each other's commitment, the sharing of our feelings begins to flow much more spontaneously, and often effortlessly. Now we can sit with the person we love and say, "You know, I had a wonderful day today. I don't know why. I think it was just because the sun was out, and that made me feel more joyful, more alive. I guess I am just happier when the sun shines." It is amazing how something as simple as the weather can affect the way we feel on any given day. Or perhaps, "I had a great day today. At our staff meeting Mr. Robinson talked about the project my team has been working on and how it is changing the industry. We needed to hear that—I needed to hear that—and his encouragement put me in a wonderful mood. It is just good to feel appreciated."

Conversely, there is something wonderfully liberating about being able to say, "You know, I am having a miserable day today. I don't know why, I just feel miserable." Sometimes it is very healthy just to accept our feelings for what they are, rather than analyzing them endlessly. Feelings don't always need a reason.

These simple exchanges can tell the people we love so much about who we are and what is going on inside us. It is a world that the people who love us desperately want to explore, but they can only do so if we allow them to. We allow the people we love into our inner world through communication. They cannot read a book about your inner life and they can't take a tour. You have to tell them about it.

Imagine taking a blind person to an art gallery and trying to describe each work of art. You couldn't just say, "This one is a Picasso"—that wouldn't convey anything of its appearance. You'd have to describe the height, the width. Is the piece a painting, a sculpture, a print, a photo? You could describe the colors, but that won't help someone who's always been blind. You must describe the art in ways a blind person can understand. Is it warm or cold? What is the texture, rough or smooth?

In the same way, we need to describe our inner world to the people with whom we are in a relationship. Don't assume that they understand what you are talking about. When it comes to each other's inner worlds, most of us are like the blind person you just took to the art gallery.

Sharing our feelings with another person can be a powerful release. Sometimes you will feel a physical weight lift from your shoulders. When the heart and the mind suffer, the body cries out. Sharing how we feel and the reasons we feel that way, or sharing how we feel even though we don't know why we feel that way, is very healthy physically, emotionally, psychologically, and spiritually.

I cannot help but marvel at the way we are all unique and independent, and at the same time, in our quest for happiness and intimacy, we could not be more interdependent. How is it that being able to say to someone we love, "I am so happy today," increases our happiness? Why is it that being able to say to someone who cares, "I feel so lonely since my father died," decreases our loneliness? I do not know and it does not matter. What is important is that whenever I can help increase another person's happiness or decrease another person's loneliness, I do.

Most of our feelings are fleeting and we know that in the grand scheme of things they are virtually insignificant; ten years from now, a specific feeling experienced at a specific time probably won't even be a blip on the screen of our relationships. But consistently being able to express these feelings *will* matter. Expressing how we feel helps those around us to know us. It is this knowledge of each other, gathered in the tiniest portions along the way, that gives rise to intimacy: to knowing and being known.

DIALOGUES OF THE DEAF

Conversations today are, for the most part, dialogues of the deaf. Everybody has something to say, but nobody is willing to listen. We observe this between husbands and wives, boyfriends and girlfriends, parents and children, employees and employers, and we also observe it between nations. There can be no intimacy in a world where nobody is willing to listen.

When people meet someone famous whom they admire, they will report something like, "I met Mother Teresa; it was amazing. I told her about what we are doing in Connecticut," or "I met the Dalai Lama and I told him about . . . ," or "I met the Pope and I told him . . . ," or "I met the President and I told him . . . ," or "I met Nelson Mandela and I told him . . ."

I always like to ask, "What did he say to you?" Usually the narrator cannot tell, either because he didn't give the famous person a chance to say anything, or because he was so consumed with what he himself was going to say that he was not listening.

If I had thirty seconds, or three minutes, with Mother Teresa, the Dalai Lama, the Pope, the President, Nelson Mandela, or any number of world leaders past and present, I wouldn't waste that time telling them anything. I would want to know what they had to tell me. Even if I disagreed considerably with some of their views or disapproved of their way of life, I have no doubt that I could learn from their extraordinary experiences. Have we become so small and selfish that even the towering figures of our age can say nothing that we think worth listening to? The truth, of course, is that every person we know, every person who crosses our path, has a wealth of experience. Learning to tap into that wealth of experience transforms conversations from exchanges of trivialities into life-changing moments.

I am also continually amazed that everyone who meets a person of considerable fame or stature, and especially a great spiritual leader, comes away saying, "It was as if nothing else in the world existed, just the two of us." In some cases, I think, this phenomenon takes place because the famous person actually has such intense focus; in other cases, I think it results because nothing else exists for *us* in that moment.

But regardless of what causes it, we all like this feeling. When was the last time you made someone feel that way? When was the last time you made your significant other (or your child) feel as if nothing else existed, just the two of you? Learning to listen will give you the power to make people feel that way.

Listening has become a lost art. We have all had this experience: we come to someone we love and trust, and we say, "I need to talk through a couple of things." Then we begin to explain our predicament, but we are interrupted within a couple of minutes by the other person saying, "What you need to do is . . ." or "Have you considered doing . . ." or "Why didn't you . . ."

The other person has assumed the role of problem solver. But chances are we don't need a problem solver. We just need someone to listen to us. In many cases, we already know what we need to do. We just needed to talk it through with someone.

The first step toward becoming a good listener revolves around the question: Why is this person saying what he or she is saying? Usually, we think becoming a good listener means focusing on what the person is saying. But *why* she is speaking is often much more important to the communication than the content of what she says. And until we know why a person is speaking, we should simply remain silent and listen. If they want you to say something, most people will ask you a question such as "So, what do you think?"

The next secret of being a great listener is to get value from your listening. I like to listen, because I never learn anything when I am speaking. I do a lot of speaking in my professional life, and in my personal life I like to do a lot of listening. It is listening that feeds and nourishes my mind, gives me new ideas, and helps me to continue to grow and change, becoming a-better-version-of-myself.

In every situation there is great value in listening, not only for the person we are listening to, but also for ourselves. And yet, the value can vary greatly from situation to situation. Take, for example, a man who goes down into a diamond mine. He knows the diamonds are there and he knows the diamonds have market value. He is searching for something of known value.

On the other hand, imagine a woman walking along the beach early one morning looking for a shell. It is the last day of a wonderful vacation, during which she and her husband have reassessed their hopes and dreams for the future, and she is searching for the perfect shell as a memento of this time together. She is not looking for something of "known value"; rather, she "finds value" in the unusual shape of the shell. If she chooses a small shell, it may make a nice pendant on a necklace, and if she chooses a larger shell it may make an elegant paperweight. Either way, she finds value.

Our listening is a very similar adventure. On the one hand, you may spend three days of your life and thousands of dollars to attend a conference where experts speak about future trends in your profession. In this case, you would be akin to the man searching for the diamond. On the other hand, you may spend an afternoon with your teenage daughter, listening to what is going on in her life. Here, you would be akin to the woman searching the beach for the shell.

There is value in everything people say, especially when the words come from someone we love and care about. Even when we disagree, there is an intrinsic value in listening. And the more we can hone the ability to listen, the more intimacy we will experience.

Being a great listener is a skill, one that we can all learn. The greatest obstacle, for most of us, is our impatience. In a world of instant messaging, online ordering, overnight delivery, and cell phones, we quickly become impatient with systems that are slower than usual, and impatient with people, who by their very nature are slower than the speed-of-light technology that surrounds us.

Earlier, I pointed out the value of virtue in relationships by explaining that two virtuous people will always have a better relationship than two unvirtuous people. Here, we unveil one of the very practical implications of that idea. Two patient people will necessarily have a better relationship than two impatient people, because their ability to listen to each other will be exponentially greater than that of their impatient counterparts. Two patient people will therefore almost certainly experience more intimacy than two impatient people.

The important thing to remember is that nobody is born patient. At birth, we are all impatient for our mother's breast and for whatever other forms of gratification we need or crave. Patience, like any other virtue, is acquired through practice.

Listening is an art that is concerned with the details. When you are listening to someone, you must move from the general to the specific. By all means, listen to the gist of what they are saying and the broad ideas they are expressing, but learn to listen, too, for the words they use. And when they use adjectives, take particular note. Adjectives are usually subjective. Adjectives will take you beyond the ideas a person is sharing and reveal how he is feeling. When someone says, "The trip was boring," he is telling you more about his feelings than about the trip. The trip was likely a wonderful opportunity, but he may have made the same trip before. Feelings are subjective, and adjectives very often reveal the feelings that lay behind the objective facts. Learn to listen for adjectives.

Other powerful tools in the art of listening include repeating back, asking questions, and asking for more information.

Repeating back to the speaker what you think he or she is saying can be a very useful tool. It shows that you have been listening, that you are interested, that you care enough to want to get it right, and that you have understood. If you have not heard the speaker correctly, it also gives her the opportunity to give further clarification.

We repeat back in order to affirm and clarify, using phrases such as "What I hear you saying is . . ." or "I think I heard you say that . . ." or "Are you saying that . . ." or "Did I understand you to say that . . ." or "Is the point you are trying to make . . ."

Questions are also an integral part of listening. They demonstrate the listener's attentiveness and interest, while allowing for clarification and further exploration of certain points.

Finally, when you are listening to someone, look at that person. When I am on the phone at home or in my office, I often find it useful to close my eyes so that I can concentrate on the conversation and not be distracted by everything around me. But eye contact is important when you are with a person. Like repeating back and asking questions, it shows that you are paying attention and that you are interested. Don't just look interested. Be interested, and as night follows day, you will look interested.

The ability to listen and the enjoyment of listening are key parts of developing intimacy. Listening is not waiting impatiently until it is your turn to speak. It is in listening that we come to know people's history, the story of their lives, their values and expectations, their opinions, their hopes and dreams. Perhaps most important, by listening we get to know how people feel and why they feel it.

Everyone loves a good listener. I know I wish I had a few more in my life.

Are you a good listener?

FEELINGS ARE REACTIONS

Feelings are a wonderful part of the human person. As our relationships grow in intimacy and we begin to form the collective ego of a team, we tend to focus more and more on positive feelings that create unity, rather than on negative feelings that create separation and isolation. Intimacy leads us to focus more on trust than on distrust, more on gratitude than on entitlement, more on appreciation than on anger.

The fifth level of intimacy is about getting comfortable with our own feelings and learning to express them to the people we love. The level of feelings is also very much about learning to listen to others, but it is also about learning to listen to ourselves, which prepares us for the seventh level of intimacy.

Feelings are extraordinary, and it is fascinating to observe how the same event can provoke such a variety of feelings in different people. Feelings often play a large role in our opinions, our values, and our choices—in many cases, a dangerously large role. Feelings can be profound and insightful, as in the case of a mother's intuition. But feelings can also be blinding and tremendously limiting, as in the case of people who are afraid of flying and refuse to take airplanes because they once saw a movie whose plot included a plane crash.

The important thing to remember about feelings is that they are a reaction. We all react differently, but it is important to know these reactions have been conditioned in us by past experience, the beliefs of friends and parents, and the general fear of change that besets the human person. Knowing that our feelings are reactions, we can train ourselves to react differently. This is no easy task, of course, but people do it every day.

Our journey toward intimacy means trying to understand why people have certain feelings and why they react to certain people and situations as they do. But, again, we will likely discover these truths about the people we love only if we restrain ourselves from judging feelings or being critical of them. Acceptance is one of the keys to further intimacy in the fifth level.

Desperate people will reveal their feelings even when they

know that they will be judged and criticized. But normally, we reveal our feelings only in the confidence that we will be accepted for who we are. We are willing to make ourselves vulnerable when we believe that we will be neither judged nor criticized but rather accepted and listened to.

Allowing the people we love to freely express their feelings is one of the greatest gifts we can give them. We all have feelings that are disordered or the result of paranoia, illusions, assumptions, and misunderstandings. It seems that the best way for the human psyche to be freed of these is the opportunity to express them in a loving and judgment-free environment, to people who truly care about us.

Tell me what you know and you entertain me, but tell me how you feel and you will intrigue me.

CHAPTER TWELVE

⚭

FAULTS, FEARS, AND FAILURES: THE SIXTH LEVEL OF INTIMACY

I NEED HELP! I'M AFRAID! I MESSED UP!

The sixth level of intimacy is the level of faults, fears, and failures. It is often here that we have to tend to the wounds of the past. Sometimes these wounds have been ignored for years, and we find them infected and festering. Cleaning our wounds can be an excruciatingly painful experience, but if we are to recover and grow strong again it cannot be avoided.

In the level of feelings (the fifth level) we certainly make ourselves vulnerable, but in the sixth level we expose ourselves. Level six is the emotional equivalent of nakedness. This emotional nakedness is usually appropriate only in our primary relationship. You may be able to expose yourself in this way to some degree in a number of your high-level relationships, but obviously it's appropriate to be around more people in your swimsuit than it is to be naked.

It is in the sixth level of intimacy that we finally let down our guard and take off our masks enough to share our faults with our significant other. He or she has known many of your faults for years, so the mere fact that you are now ready to admit to them does not produce any great advance in your relationship. The advance is made when you are willing to turn to the one you love and say honestly and humbly, "I need help."

We all do. We all need help, and a great many of our faults can only be overcome when we have help in our moments of weakness. The key, again, is acceptance and a belief that the other person has our best interests at heart. When we are convinced that our significant other is dedicated to helping us become the-best-version-of-ourselves, we become willing to lay bare our faults and ask for help.

Here, at the sixth level of intimacy, we have also finally arrived at the place where we are able to say to our significant other, "I am afraid."

I am afraid you will leave me. I am afraid we won't have enough money to retire. I am afraid I am going to lose my job. I am afraid our children will get mixed up with the wrong group of friends. I am afraid they won't get into a good college. I am afraid they won't marry for the right reasons. I am afraid of my parents dying.

Our fears are many and complex, but at the sixth level we have developed a level of comfort with our significant other that allows us to freely express them. Similarly, our partner now realizes that it is not his or her job to fix those fears, but rather to walk bravely with us.

You are right in wondering why fears are not simply included in the previous level along with all the other feelings. The reason is that fear is much more than a feeling; it is a determining factor in many of our decisions and a driving force in many other areas of our lives. For these reasons, and the others you will discover as this chapter unfolds, fear overlaps the fifth and sixth levels of intimacy.

The third component of this sixth level of intimacy is the revelation of our failures. For many of us, this is a history lesson. Your significant other probably had a good twenty or thirty years of history before he or she met you. And most of us have had some significant failures by the time we find the person we want to spend the rest of our lives with. That is not to say that we all have great shameful secrets, but we all have failures in our past. And if we look closely we will discover that those failures are affecting our present.

The sixth level of intimacy involves owning up to who we are, who we have been, what we are capable of, and how we have failed. The journey through the first five levels of intimacy empowers us and liberates us to be able to say, "I messed up!" This is a significant advance in any relationship, because if we are unable to admit that we messed up in the past, we are unlikely to be too good at admitting when we mess up today.

The ability to admit that you need help, that you are afraid, or that you messed up is a sign of great maturity in a person. The ability to accept each other's faults, fears, and failures reflects great maturity in a relationship.

DYNAMIC CHOICE MAKER OR VICTIM?

It is important to take ownership of our faults, fears, and failures because if we do not, then we become their victims. The unwillingness to admit that we need help, that we are afraid, or that we have messed up retards a person's moral, ethical, and emotional development.

The acknowledgment of our faults, fears, and failures puts

us in the position of being a dynamic choice maker. Fully aware that the past can never be changed, we are faced with a choice about the future. Are we going to continue to allow our past to determine our future, or are we going to begin to make choices that will produce a future richer and more abundant than the past?

When I say "richer," I am of course not referring to something financial (though finances may be part of it), but rather to something more exhilarating and rewarding, rich in every sense of the word and therefore rich in every aspect of your life. Most especially, I want to encourage this richness in your relationships.

If you study history, you discover that the heroes, leaders, legends, saints, and champions of every age were dynamic choice makers. They were not victims. Even religious martyrs saw themselves as choosing death and a better life. They didn't think of themselves as victims.

The sixth level of intimacy is very much about being set free from the shackles of victimhood and becoming a dynamic choice maker. When we say, "My father used to yell at me and that is why I am this way," this is the voice of a victim, not a dynamic choice maker. We have all had experiences that wounded us deeply and caused us to react to certain situations in certain ways. But we can change. That is the glory of the human person—our extraordinary ability to change, to grow, to become better-versions-of-ourselves.

Dynamic choice making is the way of all great men and women. Excellence in any field is defined by a person's ability to make dynamic choices. Mediocrity is almost always accompanied by attitudes of entitlement and victimhood.

The first step toward becoming a dynamic choice maker is taking ownership of our faults, fears, and failures.

THE DARK SIDE

In the sixth level of intimacy, we discover that we all have a dark side. We all think, say, and do things that are inconsistent with the person most people think we are and the person we are trying to be. We all think, say, and do things that are inconsistent with our core values and beliefs and the philosophy of life we are trying to follow.

The key word in all of this is "trying." We are trying to become the-best-version-of-ourselves. People often accuse me of being a hypocrite when they come face to face with one of my faults. "How can you talk and write about becoming the-best-version-of-yourself, and then do that?" they will say to me.

But the message is that we should be *striving* to become the-best-version-of-ourselves, not that I am the-best-version-of-myself and you should be, too. It is the *striving* that brings us to life; it is in *trying* that we discover our passion and purpose in life.

The question that normally follows is, When will I know that I am the-best-version-of-myself? You don't wake up one day to discover that you are now the-best-version-of-yourself, and the job is done. As you look back on your life, or upon any day in particular, there are probably moments about which you can say, "When I did that, I was the-best-version-of-myself." There are probably also a number of moments in which you know you were not the-best-version-of-yourself. In one moment, you can be your best self; in the very next moment, you can abandon that best self. It is the striving to be all we can be that animates the human person. It is the trying that breathes enthusiasm for life into us.

The point is this: we all have a dark side. Myself included.

So, everybody has a dark side, and everybody knows that everybody has a dark side, but most people go around pretending that they don't have a dark side. This is just one of the many games that we play in our social interactions with other people. In a world were nobody thinks they are average and many people think they are better than most of the people they know, is it any wonder we have trouble relating to one another?

The simplest example is this. If you take one hundred people and ask them to raise their hands if they consider themselves to be above-average drivers, more than eighty will raise their hands. Then ask everyone who considers himself an average driver to raise his hand; the rest of the one hundred people will raise their hands. Ask the same group to raise their hands if they consider themselves to be a below-average driver, and nobody will raise a hand.

I do this exercise in some of my seminars from time to time. But we all know that 80 percent of people cannot be above-average drivers, and that a significant portion of the hundred people must be below-average drivers. It is simply a statistical reality—or maybe my seminars attract only above-average drivers!

We live in our self-deceptions and they distort our character; intimacy comes to set us free from these deceptions and distortions. But in order for intimacy to do her job, we must be willing to admit to our darkness. Otherwise we will go on hiding our dark side, and the more we hide it the more powerful it will become. The more we try to hide our dark side, the more power it comes to have over us.

It is a little like alcoholism. Many alcoholics try to hide their problem, and the more they try to hide it, the more powerful it becomes. And not only that, but the more they hide their alcoholism, the more power it has over them. In time, they start to live their lives around their drinking. They plan their days around their next drink.

We, too, start to live around our darkness. It begins to direct our lives. We start to plan our days, weeks, months, and lives around our faults, fears, and failures. Until our lives become paralyzed by our darkness, until our lives simply become unmanageable.

We all have addictions, cravings, disordered desires, and an incessant selfishness, all of which constitute our dark side. They can be the chains of the past or the keys to a richer, more abundant future. The choice is ours.

The genius of intimacy is that when we bring our dark side out into the light in the context of a loving relationship, our darkness loses its power over us. Darkness cannot abide the light of love. It is intimacy that will hold our hand and walk through the dark rooms of our past and present. It is intimacy that has the power to set us free from our faults, fears, and failures.

WE ALL HAVE A PAST

There is a saying in Christian circles that every saint has a past and every sinner has a future. Some of the greatest Christian saints had very colorful pasts. The most famous for the wayward nature of his adolescence and early adult life was Augustine, who practiced no religion as a youth, lived with a mistress for fifteen years, and fathered a child prior to becoming a priest and later a bishop. In his *Confessions*, universally considered a literary masterpiece for both its remarkable theological reflections and its strikingly modern psychological insights, he wrote very frankly about his wild and misspent youth. We all have a past; we have all done things that we wish we hadn't done. This fact alone should be enough to restrain us from judging others for the blemishes in their own past.

A couple of years ago, a good friend of mine was getting married. He is one of the most genuine people I have had the pleasure of knowing, and his wife is also a remarkable person. They were very happy and I was very happy for them. But as the wedding day approached, they hit a bit of a speed bump. My friend called me about six weeks before the wedding and I could tell by his tone that all was not well, so I asked him what was going on.

It came down to this. He had had a wild youth—not over-the-top wild, but wild compared to that of his fiancée. Among his exploits had been a number of sexual encounters; his fiancée had been saving herself in this way for marriage. They had talked about their sexual histories much earlier in their relationship, and my friend had been honest with his fiancée, but as the wedding approached it became an issue.

Eventually he asked me to speak to her, which I was more than happy to do. As it turned out, her concerns were many and varied—she worried about not meeting his expectations, and she wondered how his values could have been so different in that earlier period of his life. I tried to listen to her, and when she asked me what I thought of the situation this is how I replied: "If you love him for the person he is today, then you have to realize that it is all the experiences of his past that have made him that person. If he had not had those experiences, he would not be the person he is today. If he has grown from those experiences, then he is a better man because of them, but you cannot pick and choose from a person's past between the things you like and the things you do not. However uncomfortable you are with those aspects of his past, they have contributed to making him a warm, loving, sensitive, and caring man today."

Finally, I asked her whether she had anything in her past that she wished she hadn't done. She began to blush. We all have a past.

A very important part of the sixth level is learning about the history of another person. Should we tell him or her everything? Not necessarily, and certainly not when to do so would cause great harm to her or to others. Sometimes it is enough to vaguely describe certain aspects of our past when too much detail would cause pain to those we love. But we should make an honest attempt to share our story, our personal history, the good and the bad with our significant others. Intimacy, to know and be known, is infinitely nourished in this way.

In order to encourage those we love, we must be extremely careful not to judge their past, indeed should be careful not even to appear to judge it. If we make people feel ashamed or guilty about their past, we are not worthy of their intimacy. They are already ashamed of their mistakes, just as you and I are ashamed of ours. They don't need to be reminded.

When I find myself wandering into a judgmental frame of mind, I always remind myself that if I had had the other person's experience of life and education (formal and informal) I would very likely have done the very same things, and perhaps a good deal worse. There is no place in intimacy for judgment.

We should remember that whatever a person's past, our role is to help him or her build a future. In our common quest to become the-best-version-of-ourselves, we should never allow our past to determine our future.

FORGIVENESS

This brings us to one of the most difficult topics for the human psyche and spirit. Learning to forgive those who have wronged us is very, very difficult for most of us. But the ideas that we have just discussed can help to liberate us from the destructive spirit of unforgiveness.

Unforgiveness is like drinking poison and expecting the other person to die. Unforgiveness enslaves the human spirit. Unforgiveness is the thief from our past that robs us of our future.

I have thought long and hard about forgiveness; I am not sure there are any quick tips or easy answers to the unforgiveness we often find in our hearts. But I suspect that the key to forgiving others is the realization that we have all needed forgiveness ourselves.

Forgiveness is a key component of any relationship. As we become more and more aware of our own limitations, we tend to become more and more tolerant of the limitations of other people. As we mature in this way, our self-awareness gives birth to a more spontaneous ability and willingness to forgive others. (Sometimes the real obstacle is not an inability to forgive others but our unwillingness to forgive ourselves.)

The ability to forgive is a sign of spiritual and emotional maturity, and so, too, is the ability to ask for forgiveness from those we love. And while it is important for our own development that we learn to forgive others, it does not necessarily mean that we should continue a relationship with someone who has grievously wronged us.

Sooner or later, forgiveness becomes an issue for us all. That is simply one of the consequences of having six billion wonderful but imperfect human beings inhabiting this extraordinary place we call earth.

INTIMACY AND HUMOR

It is said that the closest distance between two people is humor. Humor is a powerful and wonderful aspect of the human personality. Laughter is one of our built-in natural stress relievers. Laughter elevates the human experience by creating the lightheartedness we need to experience and enjoy life at the highest level. But there can also be a dark side to our humor, and in our relationships we need to be especially careful of this dark humor.

Our culture is preoccupied with sexual humor, as it is preoccupied with sex. I have no respect for professional comedians who use sexual innuendo and humor to get laughs. It is the easiest form of humor and usually unveils a shallow talent. Great humor gives us a new perspective on things that have been before us all along; very often, great humor is self-deprecating (though we need to be careful that we are not hiding feelings of insecurity and self-loathing in our humor).

One of the most common forms of humor is sarcasm, which can be tremendously destructive to a relationship. We have to be careful not to use humor to say the things that we need to say in the normal course of conversation. There is always a little bit of truth to humor, and that is what makes it funny. But we need to be careful not to use our humor as a code to speak to the people we love. Sarcasm is very often engaged to say something in a passive-aggressive way, when we lack the courage to face an issue in a more mature and intimate fashion.

It has been my experience that most of us are simply unaware of how often we use sarcasm and how it affects the people around us.

Sarcasm is an easy tool to use. A quick joke can break the ice during an introduction, and in this respect humor is a very powerful tool in the first and second levels of intimacy. But we have to consider the effect that humor can have on the higher levels of intimacy. It can very often be used as a dismissive tool in the third level of intimacy (opinions). Far from encouraging genuine dialogue between two people about their differing opinions, humor—and sarcasm in particular—can be a surfacing technique, returning the conversation to the shallow and safe waters of the first two levels (clichés and facts).

In and of itself, humor is neither good nor bad. As with money, television, sex, and food, what matters is how we use it. In each of the seven levels of intimacy, humor can be engaged to relieve a certain pressure and discomfort in order to further intimacy or can be used to avoid intimacy. Again, the choice is ours.

But we must not overlook the positive side of humor. Humor lifts the human spirit as few other things do, and the healthy role humor plays in relationships is very, very powerful. Being able to laugh at ourselves as individuals and as couples frees us of a self-consciousness that often prevents us from growing and thriving. Humor can be very liberating to us and our relationships, especially at times of great pressure or crisis.

We spoke earlier about how all relationships have unresolvable problems and how learning to live with these often determines whether a relationship will last. Many couples use humor to deal with their unresolvable problems. Their humor is not demeaning or accusatory, but rather is a sign of their acceptance of the other person and their unresolvable problem as a couple.

What is the secret to using humor successfully in relationships? We should use humor to increase intimacy rather than avoid it. In using humor to avoid intimacy we short-circuit a great many conversations that may be difficult, but that are necessary if we are to know and be known.

We live in a culture dominated by fear, critical of faults, and unforgiving of the imperfections that beset all of our pasts; this adds an extra challenge to our efforts to experience intimacy, and, at the same time, makes our need for genuine intimacy ever more apparent. The sixth level of intimacy is a difficult aspect of relationship to explore, but the liberation of having nothing to hide makes the discomfort and pain truly worth it. To be known, we must take off our pretenses one layer at a time and reveal the person we truly are.

The sixth level of intimacy, in which we expose our faults, fears, and failures, reveals a great deal not only about the person we are but also about what caused us to become this person. It also gives the people we love significant insight into what we need, and why. It is this understanding of each other's needs that leads us to the pinnacle of dynamic relationships, which we will now discover in the seventh level of intimacy.

CHAPTER THIRTEEN

ᏽᎾᏫᏍᎧ

LEGITIMATE NEEDS:
THE SEVENTH LEVEL
OF INTIMACY

DYNAMIC COLLABORATION

The seventh level of intimacy is where our quest to know and be known by each other turns into a truly dynamic collaboration. This final level of intimacy is the level of legitimate needs. We all have legitimate needs. If you don't eat, you will die. If you don't breathe, you will die. As we discussed earlier, these legitimate needs are most easily understood in relation to the physical realm, but we have legitimate needs in each of the four aspects of life, physical, emotional, intellectual, and spiritual.

Knowing each other's legitimate needs is a very important part of our quest to know each other in relationship. As an individual, you thrive when your legitimate needs are being met. The same is true for your significant other, your children, parents, friends, and colleagues. Having what we *want* doesn't necessarily cause us to thrive; having what we *need* causes us to thrive.

The seventh level of intimacy is not only about knowing each other's legitimate needs but also about helping each other to fulfill them.

If you have a great relationship, will your legitimate needs *always* be met? No. Sometimes things just happen, and our legitimate needs are the casualties. But this should be the exception, not the norm. When our legitimate needs chronically go unmet, we become irritable, restless, discontented, and frustrated. An individual and a relationship can endure these stressful emotions for only so long.

The seventh level of intimacy is about collaborating in the most dynamic way to know and tend to each other's legitimate needs. It is about creating a lifestyle with the person we love that is focused on the fulfillment of legitimate needs, driven by the understanding that the fulfillment of legitimate needs causes the human person to thrive . . . and causes our relationships to thrive.

Here, at the pinnacle of our quest for intimacy, we are able to share our needs with those closest to us. It is awe-inspiring to see a couple, or a family, working together to identify and fulfill each other's legitimate needs.

When you see such a relationship, you just know it enjoys a powerful intimacy. Through the acceptance of each other's different and sometimes opposing opinions (the third level), the revelation of our hopes and dreams (the fourth level), the honoring of each other's unique feelings (the fifth level), and the awareness of each other's faults, fears, and failures (the sixth level), we have learned a variety of ways to revere and celebrate the individuality of our partner. Now, in the seventh level, through the discovery of each other's legitimate needs, we can begin to build a lifestyle that helps each of us become the-best-version-of-ourselves.

Do you know what your legitimate needs are?

Do you know what your significant other's legitimate needs are?

THE FOUR ASPECTS

"Could a greater miracle take place than for us to look through each other's eyes for an instant?" was a question Thoreau once posed. This is precisely the miracle that the seventh level of intimacy concerns itself with. We look through each other's eyes, feel through each other's heart, enter each other's mind, and visit one another's soul. Even this is only the first stage of a greater miracle; the answer to Thoreau's question is yes. For once we have allowed ourselves to experience a little of life from the other person's point of view, we are in a position to know her needs and help her fulfill those needs. This is the fulfillment of the miracle that is the seventh level of intimacy: knowing and responding in a dynamic way to each other's needs.

We have already touched on the nature of our legitimate needs as individuals in each of the four aspects of the human person: physical, emotional, intellectual, and spiritual. At the beginning of part two, we discussed the idea of legitimate need in its most basic form, in relation to our physical needs. If you don't breathe, you will die: this is not difficult for us to understand, because the cause and the effect are clear. But when it comes to our legitimate needs in the other three aspects (emotionally, intellectual, and spiritual), cause and effect are not as clear, because these needs are much subtler than our physical needs.

Among your legitimate emotional needs is your need for opportunities to love and be loved. If you don't have such opportunities, you will not die as a direct result. The effects of denying our legitimate emotional needs are very subtle, but no less real. You also have a legitimate need to express your opinions, to be listened to and taken seriously, to share your feelings, and to be accepted for the person you are; you have a legitimate need for intimacy. If these legitimate emotional needs are not met, we do not die, but over time the effects are real and devastating.

Your legitimate intellectual needs are even subtler and often much more individualized. But, in general, people have a legitimate need for a variety of forms of intellectual stimulation that engage and challenge them.

Our spiritual needs are the subtlest of all. You can go for years neglecting your spiritual needs, and remain oblivious to the results of this neglect. The effect is real whether we are aware of it or not. Our most basic spiritual needs are for silence and solitude. Even people in highly functioning intimate relationships need solitude. And very often we need silence and solitude to uncover our legitimate needs in each of the four areas. More likely than not, you will not discover your deeper needs in the midst of your busy, noisy life; real reflection is required. Silence and solitude are the perfect conditions for such reflection.

In relationships, we soon realize that our legitimate needs, except for the most basic, are different from those of the people we love. For example, when faced with an important decision, a man may need time to be alone to ponder the situation, while a woman may need time with her friends to talk through it. Both needs are legitimate.

The important thing to remember about our legitimate needs in each of the four areas is that the more our lives are centered upon them the more we will thrive, and the more our relationships are centered upon them the more our relationships will thrive.

Are you thriving? Or are you just surviving? If you feel as if you are going through the motions, just getting by, then there's a good chance that a number of your legitimate needs are not being met. If you feel that your primary relationship is just surviving rather than thriving, then there is a good chance that it is not focused enough on the mutual fulfillment of legitimate needs.

If the fulfillment of our legitimate needs is so important to our happiness as individuals, and so important to our happiness as couples, why don't we focus more on it? The answer is that we get distracted, though perhaps "seduced" is a better word. Seduced by what? By our illegitimate wants. The reason is that at times our legitimate needs can seem a little drab and monotonous, while our wants can seem much more exciting and alluring.

LEGITIMATE NEEDS VERSUS ILLEGITIMATE WANTS

Modern popular culture sends the message, "Go out and get what you want from life!" This message is pressed upon us subtly and not so subtly every day of our lives, and we are encouraged to apply it to relationships along with everything else. As a result, millions of relationships are doomed even from the first moment.

The get-what-you-want philosophy cannot give birth to any form of significant or satisfying relationship for two people. It can only give birth to the selfish fulfillment of one person's desires at the expense of the other person's real and legitimate needs.

The reason is that all genuine relationships are based on giving and receiving. The very idea of an authentic relationship presupposes that you would never take pleasure or selfish fulfillment at the other person's expense. But in a culture that celebrates and applauds ruthless selfishness, such selfishness is becoming the modus operandi of more and more people in their quest to find a relationship. Needless to say, their quest is fatally flawed.

Am I saying that we should not seek personal fulfillment in relationships? No, absolutely not. I am saying that we should not seek personal fulfillment at another person's expense. And, to make a further distinction, we should be very sure not to confuse personal fulfillment with the mere satisfaction of momentary pleasures.

What is required for a relationship to develop, grow, blossom, and thrive for any significant period of time?

The answer is that we must shift our focus from the pursuit of illegitimate wants to the pursuit of legitimate needs. We have to make this shift as individuals and in our relationships as well.

Very few people today focus their lives on their legitimate needs. Most people are focused on the pursuit of their illegitimate wants. They tell themselves that when they get enough of their wants, they will be happy, fulfilled, satisfied. The reality is you simply never can get enough of what you don't really need. But we chase our illegitimate wants with reckless abandon nonetheless.

We then bring this diseased mind-set to our relationships, which we approach as if getting what we want is the goal. Now the mind games begin, and the tug-of-war between our wants and the wants of our significant other. Once this game begins it is very, very difficult to stop. We use emotional manipulation, emotional blackmail, and any number of other psychological devices to get our way. We set out to win, and we have set the game up so that winning means getting our way. It is every man and woman for themselves. It is a war between conflicting egos. The individual egos never have a chance to form a common collective ego, and so any attempt at intimacy is guaranteed to fail.

Relationships are not about getting what you want, as we have already discussed at considerable length. Relationships are about helping each other to become the-best-version-of-ourselves. Wants play a very small role. Needs, on the other hand, are of paramount importance.

Sooner or later, we all come to a fork in the road of our lives as individuals: we have to decide whether we will base our lives on the pursuit of our legitimate needs or on the pursuit of our wants. As couples we have to make the same decision about our relationships.

If we choose our wants, then we are signing the death certificate of our relationship. It may last another year or two, it may even last another ten years. But it cannot thrive with the pursuit of individual wants as its focus. The goal of such a relationship is set against the very nature of relationship.

If, on the other hand, you are willing to set your individual desires aside and give first priority to your legitimate needs and the legitimate needs of the one you love, then you find yourself at the beginning of what could become a dynamic collaboration.

Turn your attention away from your wants and desires (which are usually selfish and driven by ego) toward your legitimate needs, and your life will change forever. Redirect the focus of your relationship away from your individual wants and desires and toward the legitimate needs of your partner and yourself, and your relationship will change forever.

You may have noticed that up until this point I have made very little direct mention of love, though I have, of course, been speaking about it indirectly at every turn. At this point, I would like to pose a question for us to consider.

What is love?

How do you know when you love someone?

How do you know when another person loves you?

Love is the wanting, and the having, and the choosing, and the becoming. Love is a desire to see the person we love be and become all he or she is capable of being and becoming. Love is a willingness to lay down our own personal plans, desires, and agenda for the good of the relationship. Love is delayed gratification, pleasure, and pain. Love is being able to live and thrive apart, but choosing to be together.

You know you love somebody when you are willing to subordinate your personal plans, desires, and agenda to the good of the relationship.

You know another person loves you when he or she is willing to subordinate his or her personal plans, desires, and agenda to the good of the relationship.

At times, you must be willing to give up your wants so that his or her needs can be fulfilled. Sometimes you may even be required to forgo your own real and legitimate needs, so that his or her needs can be met. Are you willing?

Are you willing to suffer for love? How much are you willing to suffer in order to have a truly amazing relationship? Are you prepared to let go of all your whims, cravings, and fancies, in order to pursue something more mundane, something simpler?

Most people are not, and that's okay. But you cannot expect to drink the emotionally thirst-quenching waters of real intimacy if you are unwilling to make the arduous journey into the mountains where those waters spring forth. If you are not willing to pay the price, then you must stay in the emotional cities and drink your bottled water. The springs of intimacy are not for emotional tourists; they are for those committed to knowing and being known.

Intimacy is a mountaintop experience. Its pinnacle is the dynamic collaboration between two people to see to it that each other's legitimate needs are fulfilled. This requires constant attention. You cannot put such a relationship on autopilot. We must constantly be honing our ability to recognize the needs of those we love, even when they are unable to articulate those needs.

LEARNING THE LANGUAGE OF NEEDS

Creating a lifestyle as a couple that attends to these legitimate needs is no easy task. Most people have a hard enough time working out what their own legitimate needs are, never mind trying to discover the needs of those they love. In order to further this dynamic fulfillment of our legitimate needs, we have to learn the language of our needs and the language of our partner's needs.

People don't always say what they want, people don't always say how they feel, and people rarely say what they need. Much of our relating is done by reacting to each other and to the people, things, and events around us. When we are simply reacting we are in a defensive mode, and either standing still or moving backwards.

The genius of the seventh level of intimacy is that it teaches us to act rather than react. This difference may seem slight or simple, but in the course of our daily lives, and especially in our relationships, it can have an enormous impact. If we can learn to speak and understand the language of needs we will no longer find ourselves discussing or quietly resenting our unfulfillment, but will find that our conversations turn to how we can help each other fulfill our legitimate needs in the future.

The first step is to overcome the foolish notion that our mates should know what we need and when we need it.

Jim has had a tough day. His boss was in from the head office for the day and was nothing but critical of the way Jim is running the regional office. Throughout the day, Jim kept himself going with the thought "I can't wait to get home, eat a good meal, and just relax watching the basketball game." But when he arrives home, his wife, Susan, announces that tonight they are going to finalize the guest list for their daughter's wedding. Jim immediately becomes uncooperative, resentful, and moody. Susan thinks this is about the invitation list, but of course it has nothing to do with that.

Jim knew what he needed, but he failed to communicate it. It would have been easy enough for him to pick up the phone midafternoon and tell Susan, "Listen, honey, I'm having a very stress-filled day. I really need to just enjoy a quiet meal with you tonight and relax." Had he done so, his wife would be aware of his needs. But without this communication she has no idea that he has had a tough day at the office.

On any other day, Jim might bound through the door full of energy, expecting Susan to be ready to go running with their dog as they usually do. But on this particular day she has had an argument with a friend and isn't in the mood to do much but sit and talk through her hurt. Jim won't know that unless she tells him. All it takes is a phone call to say, "Jim, I really need to just sit and talk this evening when you get home. I don't feel like running with the dog and I can't muster the energy to cook dinner."

Now Jim knows her needs. "No problem. We can just sit around and have a drink and talk, and then I'll cook us up something for dinner. Or, if you'd prefer, we could just order a pizza!"

These are examples of needs that emerge from circumstances, but perhaps more important to know and understand are our everyday needs.

The simplest things can radically affect our effectiveness in relationships and our happiness in general. For example, if I don't get eight hours' sleep more than a couple of nights in a row, I become irritable, moody, easily distracted, and generally ineffective. My need for sleep is legitimate, and my staff and the people I love know that I shouldn't be kept up late or scheduled too early unless absolutely necessary.

Over the years I have also become aware of how demanding life on the road can be for my staff. It has become apparent that when the schedule becomes busier and more stressful, my staff's need for exercise increases. An adrenaline-pumped hour each afternoon can make all the difference six weeks into a speaking tour. I know they need it to thrive; it is my job to see that they have it, and to encourage them to push themselves when they would rather just take an hour nap.

This is seventh-level intimacy: knowing, recognizing, and honoring each other's legitimate needs. This is the pinnacle of relations between husband and wife, boyfriend and girlfriend, parents and child, employee and employer, and in any other relationship that you deem worthy of intimacy.

The seventh level is not about you fulfilling your partner's needs and neglecting your own. It is about the gentle, and sometimes not so gentle, give and take of sharing, knowing, and striving to fulfill each other's needs. This seventh level requires a thoughtfulness that is beyond ego-driven behavior.

Here in the seventh level we see the culmination of all that we have learned and discovered about ourselves and each other throughout the process.

The first level taught us about clichés. In the seventh level we recognize that when someone we love resorts to clichés, something is wrong—there is a need, a hurt, or a barrier that must be addressed.

The second level taught us to honor each other's personal history, and to be continually trying to learn more about each other's lives before we met and more about the time we have spent apart since we met.

The third level taught us to accept each other despite differing opinions and expectations. This acceptance opened the door to the deep levels of intimacy, by allowing us to be comfortable sharing our hopes and dreams, our feelings, and our faults, fears, and failures.

The simplicity of the model can be deceiving, in that we may not realize how far we have come or how much has been covered in each of these seven levels. But the carefree timelessness that allows us to move from the first to the second level also enriches every level along the way.

The sharing of our personal facts and history, which allows us to move beyond the mundane aspect of level two, also helps us to understand something about why we feel what we feel, dream what we dream, fear what we fear, and need what we need.

Level three teaches us how to agree and disagree in ways that bring life to our relationships, rather than destroying enthusiasm and creating resentments. The acceptance that breaks down our prejudices and biases in level three helps us to recognize that we are all at different places in the journey and prepares us to love each other for where we are right now. This allows us to set aside our individual egos and form a collective ego, and now the real journey together begins.

Realizing that our fates are connected, we then learn in level four how important it is to set aside selfish desire if our collective hopes and dreams are to be realized. But we also discover the need for individual hopes and dreams and how to help each other pursue these. Most of all, the wisdom of the fourth level affirms that no worthy dream can be achieved without a willingness to delay gratification at some points along the way.

The power of being vulnerable and learning to express our feelings in ways that are healthy to us as individuals is the gift of the fifth level.

The sixth level of intimacy encourages the wisdom to admit our faults and failings in order to build a richer and more abundant future. Here, we also learn the importance of forgiving others, accepting forgiveness from other people, and forgiving ourselves.

At every step along the way, we are creating a more cohesive lifestyle, one that allows us to thrive as individuals and that allows our relationships to thrive. In many ways, the first six levels provide the tools for us to be able to communicate and participate in each other's lives in a way that truly helps both of us become the-best-versions-of-ourselves.

In the seventh level of intimacy, we recognize that it is not what we want that is most important, but rather what we need. Only then, enriched by the wisdom of the seventh level, do we actively stop seeking the attainment of our illegitimate wants and begin to genuinely pursue the fulfillment of our legitimate needs.

This collaboration that leads two people to create a lifestyle focused on the mutual fulfillment of legitimate needs is the incarnation of intimacy. With our backs turned on the philosophy of "What's in it for me?" and our hearts set on the philosophy of "How can I help you to become all you were created to be?," our relationships become flooded with thoughtfulness. And where two thoughtful people come together to honor and help each other, there you will find a deep and abiding love.

Though at times they are the result of unreasonable expectations, anger, resentment, discontentedness, and frustration are often signs that our needs are not being met. Learn to listen to your anger, frustration, and stress. They are trying to tell you something. Is there an unmet legitimate need crying out from within them?

The seven levels of intimacy constitute a wonderful adventure, one that we are constantly taking. Every time we enter one of the levels it seems new and different, because we are new and different since we were last there. Our needs change and our dreams change, our feelings and opinions change, and as they do, so does the world around us.

There is a saying in the Talmud: "Every blade of grass has its angel that bends over it and whispers, 'Grow, grow.' " That is what I hope to be to the people I love: an angel of encouragement. That is what I hope the seven levels of intimacy will be for you: an angel of encouragement. That is what I hope you will be to others: an angel of encouragement.

From time to time, we all need to be encouraged. It is encouragement from those we love that gives us courage when we are afraid, hope when we are in despair, light when it appears that darkness will prevail, faith when we are consumed by doubt, joy when it seems that sorrow has overcome us, and peace when unrest holds our hearts hostage.

PART THREE

CHAPTER FOURTEEN

༄༅

TEN REASONS PEOPLE DON'T HAVE GREAT RELATIONSHIPS

WHO WANTS A GREAT RELATIONSHIP?

W ho would say no to a great relationship? Everyone wants one, but only a rare few ever experience it. Ever year, tens of thousands of young men dream of playing basketball for an NBA team, but less than one-tenth of one percent ever realize their dream. Most people would like to be wealthy, and still, 10 percent of Americans own and control 90 percent of U.S.-traded stocks.

The first time I read the following, I was amazed. It is the last line of what is considered Spinoza's greatest work, his *Ethics*. Spinoza was a seventeenth-century Jewish-born Dutch philosopher. While I certainly don't agree with all he wrote, the last line of this work offers an insight that is astoundingly enlightening to all those who strive to succeed in any field:

"All great things are as difficult to achieve as they are rare to find."

This is the great truth we often overlook when we gaze upon extraordinary success. Great wealth is as difficult to achieve as it is rare to find; that is why only a few possess it. Great sporting talent is as difficult to achieve as it rare to find; that is why only a few possess it and hundreds of thousands gather to watch them display it. Great relationships are as difficult to achieve as they are rare to find; and that is why, while we would all like to have one, so few ever experience any measure of a truly great relationship.

Behind all great success, you find men and woman with a greater desire and discipline than the rest. One of the reasons people don't have great relationships is not because they don't want one; it's just that they don't want it badly enough.

But there is no one reason why people don't have great relationships. Let's take a look at ten reasons. You will discover that they are quite simple, which is very often the reason we overlook or neglect them. They are prescriptions that are very often misplaced in the middle of a culture that worships complexity. Does your life need any more complexity? Does your relationship need any more complexity? Our lives are in desperate need of a little simplicity.

Many people say they want love, but they actually do everything in their power to avoid it. Many people say that they want intimacy desperately, but they actually do everything in their power to avoid it. Many, many people say that they desperately want a great relationship while doing everything in their power to avoid or sabotage one.

Let's take a look at 10 reasons people don't have a great relationships.

The Ten Reasons

Reason 1: They Don't Establish a Common Purpose

Most people meet someone, become infatuated, fall in love, date, and marry, without ever taking the time to discuss or explore the purpose of their relationship. As a result, they are constantly disoriented in their relationship, which is always being driven to and fro by the conflicting and competing winds of individual egos and selfish desires.

Our essential purpose is the foundation upon which we build a life filled with passion and purpose. You are here to become the-best-version-of-yourself. This essential purpose also provides the common purpose for every relationship, which is to help each other become the-best-versions-of-ourselves. It doesn't matter if the relationship is between husband and wife, parent and child, friend and friend, neighbor and neighbor, or business executive and customer. The first purpose, obligation, and responsibility of a relationship is to help each other achieve our essential purpose.

"The most empowering relationships are those in which each partner lifts the other to a higher possession of their own being." —Pierre Teilhard de Chardin

Reason 2: They Don't Clearly Define What Makes a Relationship Great

We have diverse visions and different ideas about what makes a great relationship. Most people never define what it would take for them to feel that they have a great relationship. As a natural consequence, they never find that relationship. If you don't know what you are looking for, you will never find it. Worse still, even if you do find it, you will not recognize it.

Often, another person's primary relationship may seem fantastic to you or me. We may even be quietly envious of it. But the person we envy is dissatisfied, even miserable. Why? Because we all have differing visions of what makes up a great relationship.

What's your vision of a great relationship?

What would it take for you to be fulfilled in your relationship?

When you ask most people these questions, they either can't say or they give some random and superficial answer. The reality is, they have never taken the time to think this through.

"The thing has already taken form in my mind before I begin. The first attempts are absolutely unbearable. I say this because I want you to know that if you see something worthwhile in what I am doing, it is not by accident but because of real direction and purpose." —Vincent Van Gogh

Reason 3: They Make It a Moving Target

No plan, no purpose, just a moving target. There is no chance of finding fulfillment in this scenario, only dissatisfaction. When we don't take the time to establish what makes a great relationship for us, we are constantly window shopping. Driven by our whims, cravings, ego, and self-centered interests, our vision of what makes a great relationship changes every day.

Under these circumstances, we are never satisfied, we keep moving the goalposts, and this creates enormous dissatisfaction in us and a great frustration in our partner. It would be as if we were playing football, and just after the play has taken place the end zone was moved. It would be as if every time you kicked, the goalposts were moved while the ball was still in the air.

Is your relationship constantly trying to hit a moving target?

This is why it is so important to step back for a moment, look at the big picture, and take your time in formulating your vision of a great relationship.

It goes without saying that we will always keep changing and growing, always striving to better ourselves, but there has to be a point where we can say, "We've got a great relationship." There have to be times of celebration as our relationships improve. There have to be times of gratitude for the distance that has been covered, for the changes that have been achieved. At these times we are able to say, "Let's continue to fine-tune our relationship. We have a really good thing; let's do whatever it takes to sustain it."

Without a clearly defined purpose for their relationship, and in the absence of any real plan, most people are set up for disappointment. Without the focus that a purpose and plan bring to our lives and relationships, most people become irritable, restless, and discontented. The reason is that without a commonly agreed upon purpose and plan we become disoriented, and everything becomes a moving target.

"It's a sad day when you find out that it's not accident, or time, or fortune, but just yourself that kept things from you." —Lillian Hellman

Reason 4: They Make It Seem Impossible

The fourth reason most people don't have great relationships is that they make it seem impossible. They define a great relationship in unrealistic terms—for example, as one where a couple never argues, or has no unresolvable problems.

People with this unrealistic vision have forgotten that their significant other is first and foremost an individual with likes and dislikes, with preferences and opinions, with a past that is rich in experiences and education that may be vastly different from their own. Above all, they have forgotten that no human being is perfect or programmable.

If you define a great relationship as one without any unresolvable problems, or one without any conflict, then you are setting yourself up for frustration and disappointment. You may convince yourself that your significant other is the cause of your frustration, but you are the cause of your own frustration. Your frustration is the fruit of your misguided expectations. Your frustration represents the gap between your unrealistic expectations and imperfect reality.

Strive to become the-best-version-of-yourself and strive to have a great relationship, but make allowances in your planning and goal setting for the wondrous imperfections and limitations of the human person.

"A great deal of talent and opportunity is lost to the world for want of a little courage. Every day sends to their graves obscure men whose timidity prevented them from making a first effort." — Sydney Smith

Reason 5: They Don't Believe

We live in an age when many people believe that faith is impractical and sentimental. The truth is we live by faith, and cannot live long without it. Most of us drive down the road every day. We have faith that the people driving in the other direction will stay on their side of the road. Our lives are filled with thousands of these simple beliefs, and they make our lives work. If we didn't believe, if we didn't have faith that the oncoming drivers would indeed stay on their side of the road, we would be paralyzed by fear. Fear is the natural response to the absence of faith, and indeed, the result of the absence of faith.

The fifth reason people don't have great relationships is that they make their vision of what makes a great relationship so grand

and unrealistic that they never really *believe* that they can achieve it, so they don't even try. It all seems too hard, too high, and too far. "Why bother?" they say to themselves. These are often the cynics, the skeptics, and the critics.

Create a vision. Establish the purpose of your relationship. Commit to a plan that is realistic and commonly agreed upon. Believe. For without belief no good thing was ever accomplished.

"Faith is an excitement and an enthusiasm: it is a condition of intellectual magnificence to which we must cling as to a treasure . . . one that should never be squandered." —George Sand

Reason 6: They Never Make It an Absolute Must

If you needed a great relationship to survive, you would have one. If you needed a relationship the way you need air to breathe or water to drink, you would be in a great relationship right now. Most people are more interested in simply surviving than they are in thriving. Most people have what they *must* have, not what they would like to have.

Reason number six is that they never make it an absolute must to have a great relationship. If you took a few minutes to sit down and write out all the ways a great relationship would cause you to flourish and thrive, then establishing such a great relationship would likely become significantly more important to you. If you keep pondering the ways a great relationship would transform you and your life, at some point you would come to the conclusion that you must have a great relationship.

Those who never reflect in this way live their lives thinking or saying, "I wish I had a great relationship," or "It would be nice to have a great relationship," or "I hope that happens to me one day." They describe people who have great relationships as lucky. They never make it an absolute must to have a great relationship.

Great relationships are as difficult to achieve as they are rare to find. They are not achieved by luck or chance. They don't just show up and are never convenient. Couples with great relationships decide that they are unwilling to live without a dynamic collaboration. They make it a must. They treasure their relationship above all the fleeting and superficial things that most of us give our time and attention to, for they realize that a dynamic relationship causes them to thrive in the emotional aspect of their lives, and encourages and challenges them to thrive in the physical, intellectual, and spiritual aspects. They have discovered their natural yearning for intimacy, and they are living out the dream of that intimacy.

You've got the relationship you must have, not the one you should have, or the one you'd like to have. Only when you realize that you can't live and thrive without a great relationship will you seriously begin to take steps toward establishing one. You've got to make it a must!

" 'Come to the edge,' he said. They said, 'We are afraid.' 'Come to the edge,' he said again. They came. He pushed them . . . and they flew." —Guillaume Apollinaire

Reason 7: They Don't Follow Through

Some people never have a great relationship because they create an unrealistic plan. Others fail even though they have a realistic plan, and the reason is that they simply don't follow through.

Every year, millions of people make New Year's resolutions, and more than 90 percent of them fail to keep these resolutions for the first month of the year. Some fail because their plan is unrealistic, but most fail because they simply don't follow through. Most people have a fairly good sense of what new habits would significantly impact their lives in a healthy way. They make resolutions, but fail to transform the resolutions into habits.

We don't follow through for a plethora of reasons, but usually they boil down to the fact that we just don't want it badly enough. We put off having a great relationship. We attend to other things of relative insignificance and ignore the plan we made that would help us create a great relationship.

"I have never known a really successful man who deep in his heart did not understand the grind, the discipline it takes to win." —Vince Lombardi

Reason 8: They Have No Accountability

A wonderful and difficult part of intimacy is holding each other accountable. Accountability is wonderful because it is a relational tool that forcefully propels a person along the path toward the-best-version-of-himself or herself. Accountability is an extraordinary stimulus to the improvement of the human person. Whether it is on the football field or in relationships, accountability has a mysterious way of bringing the best out of people. At the same time, accountability is a very difficult aspect of intimacy. It takes great love and courage to hold a person accountable. I say "love" because accountability is one of the best ways we can help others to become the-best-version-version-of-themselves. I say "courage" because it is often easier to overlook a situation where a person has betrayed, or is about to betray, his or her best self.

The eighth reason people don't have great relationships is that they have no accountability in their relationships. They stay out of each other's business, so to speak. Intimacy is about being involved, intimately, with each other's business.

Many couples formulate a plan, but fail because they are unwilling to hold each other accountable to the plan, or unwilling to be held accountable to it themselves.

The truth is, this is one of the most common reasons we don't put together a plan to begin with. With a plan come responsibility and accountability, and the selfish and lazy part of each and every single one of us despises responsibility and accountability. The lazy and selfish part cries out for spontaneity and freedom, distorting these wonderful qualities in order to deflect responsibility and avoid accountability.

There are people who want to be in a relationship, but don't want to be in a relationship. Let me translate: they want to be in a relationship, but they don't want intimacy. They want the convenience and security of having someone around, because otherwise they would be alone, and that would force them to face up to their miserable and pathetic selves. So they avoid being alone at all costs. Instead, they inflict their miserable and pathetic self on someone else, even though they have no real intention of establishing true intimacy. These people will very often avoid and abandon anyone who attempts to hold them accountable.

We all need accountability. It keeps us honest and brings the best out of us. It is a prerequisite for all intimate relationships. People who avoid accountability should themselves be avoided in intimate relationships.

I suggested during our discussion of building a future together that, having established your common purpose, formulated your plan, and had your first dream-making weekend or sessions, you set a date one year away on which you will assess how you are doing. That holds you accountable. For the same reason, I suggested you write down your purpose, goals, dreams, and plan. It keeps you accountable.

"It should be the effort of each to ease and enrich the life of the other. In this way each is safe. Each feels that he is worthwhile; each feels that he is needed." —Alfred Adler

Reason 9: They Give Up in the Face of Major Challenges

Times of great triumph and celebration rarely improve the character of a person. Good character is usually formed in the furnace of life's great struggles and challenges. And so it is with relationships. It is easy to be together when everything is wonderful, but our togetherness is tested when life's trials come knocking on the door of our relationships.

Recently I had breakfast with a dear friend. The past five or six years have been a time of painful growth for her and her family. About six years ago, her husband confided in her that he hated his job and that he felt like he was leading a life of quiet desperation.

My friend had seen his enthusiasm for life slowly draining out of him over the eighteen months preceding his confession, and she didn't like what it was doing to their relationship or the family. She immediately encouraged him to look for another job; he did so, and soon found one that he thought would bring him greater fulfillment. But almost immediately, he realized that it would be little different from the one he had left. Burdened and troubled by his financial responsibilities—they have four children—he began to despair. They talked more about it as a couple, and my friend encouraged him to go away for a weekend retreat to really think about what he wanted to do.

When he returned, he announced that he would like to start his own business. Ever supportive, she encouraged him. They took a second mortgage on their house and she began to work more at her part-time job to bring in a little extra money during the start-up phase. Only this start-up phase dragged on, and on, and on. All the while, financial pressure was building on this couple. The husband would lie awake at night worrying about it. In the middle of the day, when he was at work and the children were at school, the wife would cry her eyes out, wondering what was going to happen. But all along they talked about it, encouraged each other, and promised each other that they would get through this and that things would work out.

The business never did make it past the start-up phase, and my friend's husband found himself looking for a job again. This time he found a wonderful job, with a wonderful company, doing something he loves, with people who are a joy to work with. He feels he is making a contribution, his employers make him feel appreciated, and he is earning good money. But what a journey that family has been through.

At breakfast my friend said to me, "I am so proud of him. So many men live their whole lives in that misery and never do anything about it. But he had the courage to stand up and step out and improve his life. It has been tough, but we made it through, and I wouldn't change it. It has made him a better man, it has made us a better couple, and it has made us a better family."

It is often the times of great struggle that make us stronger and strengthen the bonds of intimacy. Couples that have great relationships are not the ones that never experience tough challenges, but those that face them together bravely.

The ninth reason that people don't have great relationships is that they give up when they face major challenges.

"Be patient toward all that is unresolved in your heart. And try to love the questions themselves. Do not seek the answers that cannot be given you because you would not be able to live them. And the point is to live everything. Live the questions now. Perhaps you will then gradually, without noticing it, live along some distant day into the answer." —Rainer Maria Rilke

Reason 10: They Never Get Quality Coaching

We learn everything from the people with whom we share this world. We learn how to walk by watching others walk. We learn how to talk by hearing others talk. We learn how to ride a bicycle by being taught how to ride a bicycle. Other people instruct us, tell us what we are doing wrong, and encourage us to keep trying. This sort of coaching is invaluable in any human endeavor. What makes us think it wouldn't be just as valuable in our quest to be part of a great relationship?

The final reason most people never have a great relationship is because they never get quality coaching.

Good coaching is available in thousands of different forms and methods. You are being coached right now. Books change our lives. Books expand our vision of ourselves, and our vision of the world. And good books about relationships expand our vision of relationship.

You may not always have the time to read, so pick up one audio book about relationships each month for the next twelve months. Listen to the books while you are driving around. It's simple, it's easy, and you will be amazed by how that one new habit will transform your relationships. How? Not because audio programs are magical, but because human thought is creative: what we think becomes. Whatever you place your attention upon will increase in your life.

Another way to get coaching is to go to a couples counselor. I realize that most people only go to marriage counselors when they have a problem, and you might not have a problem. Perhaps therein lies the problem. Maybe, just maybe, we need this valuable coaching before it is too late. Most people who have been through marriage counseling wish they had seen a counselor before they had a problem. And a great many say they would never have had the problem if they had known what they learned through counseling. How rare do you think it is for a marriage counselor to see a couple that is just trying to improve their marriage? It almost never happens. People come for counseling only when they are ready to divorce or cannot stand to be in the same room with each other anymore.

Retreats and seminars are also a great way to expose your relationship to new ideas and coaching. Ideas change the world. There are any number of examples of this truth. From Plato to Aquinas, from Einstein to Darwin, ideas have been changing the world and the way we live in it. Ideas also change our lives and our relationships. We should make it a priority to constantly feed and fuel our minds with great ideas. Retreats and seminars are an excellent source of new ideas and also a wonderful place to meet others who are trying to improve themselves and their relationships.

The most powerful sources of coaching in relationships are other couples who have great relationships. We learn more from our friends than we ever will from books. Surrounding ourselves with couples who have great relationships exposes us to the ways they relate and interact. By being with couples who have extraordinary relationships, we learn about the love and consideration that nurture true intimacy. This may mean that we will have to expand our circle of friends to include couples much older than we are, for they are usually the ones who have refined the art of loving and the joy of being loved.

Coaching is powerful in every aspect of our lives. Find a coach, or a number of coaches, for whatever areas of your life you want to improve. Don't overlook coaches who are available through books and tapes, or as presenters at seminars or retreats. Some of your coaches may be friends or professionals. Coaching is invaluable in our quest to become the-best-version-of-ourselves, and we should not overlook the power of coaching in helping us to establish a great relationship.

"Someday, after we have mastered the winds, the waves, the tide and gravity, we shall harness for God the energies of love. Then, for the second time in the history of the world, man will have discovered fire." —Pierre Teilhard de Chardin

INVERT AND MULTIPLY

There you have the main reasons most people never have a great relationship. For the most part, they are disarmingly simple. And their inverse is, too. Invert them, and you will discover ten reasons some people do have great relationships.

Reason 1: They Establish a Common Purpose

Reason 2: They Clearly Define What Makes a Relationship Great

Reason 3: They Agree on a Plan to Establish a Great Relationship

Reason 4: Their Plan Is Realistic

Reason 5: They Believe They Can Achieve Their Goal

Reason 6: They Make It an Absolute Must to Be Part of a Great Relationship

Reason 7: They Persevere and Follow Through

Reason 8: They Hold Each Other Accountable to Their Purpose and Plan

Reason 9: They Don't Give Up in the Face of Major Challenges

Reason 10: They Get Quality Coaching

Vaclav Havel, the Czech dramatist and human rights activist who later became his country's president, wrote, "I believe that nothing disappears forever, and less so deeds, which is why I believe that it makes sense to try to do something in life, something more than that which will bring one obvious returns." What could be more worthy of your life than to apply yourself to the task of building a handful of truly beautiful relationships?

CHAPTER FIFTEEN

❧

DESIGNING A GREAT RELATIONSHIP

THOSE WHO FAIL TO PLAN . . .

Napoleon wrote, "Those who fail to plan can plan to fail."
When I speak to audiences around the world about relationships, I like to begin by asking, "Raise your hand if you don't want to have a great relationship!"

No one ever does.

People want great relationships, but for all the reasons we have just discussed, millions of people find themselves in mediocre relationships and starved for intimacy. Throughout the book I have tried to emphasize the importance of placing our essential purpose at the center of our lives and at the center of our relationships. This is first among the factors critical for success in relationships. The second critical success factor is formulating a plan. In the previous chapter we discussed the theory behind formulating a plan. In this chapter I would like to approach the plan in a more practical and personal way.

Michael Jordan once commented in an interview, "I visualized where I wanted to be, what kind of player I wanted to become. I knew exactly where I wanted to go, and I focused on getting there." Behind every great success story there was a plan.

Do you think Ralph Lauren just starts cutting the material for his clothes without a plan? No. He begins by making sketches. From the sketches he comes up with a design. From the design he starts cutting the material. Does he make mistakes? Absolutely. Does the design need to be modified from time to time? Of course it does. The sketches are his plan.

People rarely enter relationships in order to break up. People don't get married to get divorced. I suspect that most people getting married believe that they will be together forever. And yet more than half of marriages today end in divorce or separation. People don't fail because they want to fail. People don't plan to fail, they simply fail to plan, and those who fail to plan can plan to fail.

So if you are really serious about having a great relationship, you have to come up with a plan.

The Ultimate Partner

Imagine you are single again. If you are single, no imagination required. What does a great relationship look like to you? Most people don't know what they want in a relationship, so they end up with whatever comes along. Knowing what you want is critical to the planning process.

Now many of you may be thinking, I already have a relationship and I am stuck in it, so what's the point of imagining that I am single? Sometimes designing without constraints helps us to see what is really important to us, just as dreaming without limits expands our horizons. In the same way, even if you are in a relationship, imagining that you're single will enable you to see more clearly what you are looking for in a partner and how you may want to transform your existing relationship.

So, imagining that you are single, write down all the qualities you would like your ideal partner to possess. With your ideal partner in mind, answer the following questions:

> What would the physical traits and level of health of your
>   ideal partner be?
> What are some of the emotional qualities that your ideal
>   partner would possess?
> What intellectual characteristics would your ideal partner
>   display?
> What spiritual beliefs and practices would your ideal partner
>   have?
> What would the professional life of your ideal partner involve?
> What are his or her hobbies, interests, passions, values, and
>   beliefs?

What did you come up with? Most people have a very clear idea of what they don't want, but find it hard to describe what they do want. But the more you are able to describe what you are looking for, the better your chance of attracting that to your relationship.

There are thousands of qualities you could assign to your ideal spouse, and of course nobody is going to have every one of them (especially not if you have 384 qualities on your list). So, the next step in designing a great relationship is to go through the list of qualities you would like your ideal partner to have and identify those that are nonnegotiable.

Here are some examples of qualities that people have proposed as nonnegotiable in their ideal partners: "integrity," "someone who takes care of himself or herself," "a person who looks great whether she is dressed to the nines or in sweats and a T-shirt," "adventurous," "a sense of humor," "active in the community," "well-read," "open-minded," "curious," "spiritual," "a good listener," "nonjudgmental," "someone who wants to make a difference," "someone who wants to be a mother," "someone who wants to be a father," "intelligent," "handyman," "likes the outdoors," "lives in X city."

The possibilities are endless! The question is, Which qualities are nonnegotiable for you? List the nonnegotiable qualities you would be looking for in a partner if you were single today.

Have you ever noticed that when you are thinking of buying a particular car, you start to see that car everywhere? This happens because you are focusing on that model, and whatever we give our mental attention to will increase in our lives. We attract to our lives whatever we think about. If we think about the negative, it is the negative we attract. If we think about positive things, it is positive things that we attract. If we think about scarcity, it is scarcity that we attract. And if we think about abundance, it is abundance that we attract. If we think about all the things that we don't want in a relationship, we attract the things that we don't want. If we think about what we are looking for in a relationship, we attract the kind of relationship we are looking for. This is why it is so important to be clear about what we are looking for in a relationship. There are few things more powerful than a clear vision. Once you know what you are looking for, you will be amazed how quickly it appears.

Now let's take a look at what the ultimate relationship looks like for you.

THE ULTIMATE RELATIONSHIP

What does the ultimate relationship look like for you? How would you treat each other? How would you spend your time together? How do you make each other feel? Again, the more specific you can be the better. Hazy goals produce hazy results. A clear vision is the first step in creating an extraordinary relationship.

Returning to our example of purchasing, or thinking of purchasing, a car. If you just say to yourself, "I want to buy a new car," you will not raise your consciousness to attract any particular car. Specific intentions produce specific results. Try to describe your ultimate relationship in as much detail as possible.

Again, there are thousands of possibilities. For you the ultimate relationship may include exercising together, cooking together, traveling together, holding each other accountable, praying together, being comfortable expressing affection in public, raising children, taking summer courses at a local college together, taking annual camping trips, continuing a family Thanksgiving tradition, going to church together, helping each other become the-best-version-of-yourselves. There is no end to the possibilities.

So having designed the ultimate partner, now take some time and design the ultimate relationship.

THE CURRENT REALITY

Now let's look at your existing relationship. If you are single at this time, you may want to do this exercise with your last significant relationship in mind. If that is too painful, choose a relationship that is more comfortably placed in your past.

Being brutally honest with yourself and about yourself, your partner, and your relationship is critical to this exercise. With your existing relationship in mind, answer the following questions.

What are your significant other's ten best qualities?

Describe ten ways you would like to see your significant other become a-better-version-of-himself or herself.

If you could change three things about your relationship with each other, what would they be?

What effect would these changes have on your relationship?

Do you think your significant other is aware of the advantage of changing these things?

Have you spoken about these things in a positive and proactive way?

Describe ten ways you think your significant other would like you to become a-better-version-of-yourself.

If your significant other is willing to go through the process of answering these questions also, you will have the basis for some very, very healthy conversations. I suggest that he or she read the book first, so that he or she understands the context of designing the ultimate relationship. If your significant other is uncooperative or just unwilling to participate, that may say something about his or her commitment to your relationship or about the way you asked; then again, you may just have caught him or her at the wrong moment.

DESIGNING A GREAT RELATIONSHIP

If your significant other is willing to read this book and partici-pate, celebrate that. In and of itself, it is a sign of a willingness to build a richer and more abundant future together. In the spirit of cooperation, you are now ready to design a great relationship.

Up until now, we have simply been brainstorming in order to

understand a little more deeply and consciously what moves us, what drives us, and what is important to us. Now we can move into the actual design phase and then on to the planning and implementation phase.

If you have not already done so, get each other a journal. Go to the bookstore together, pick out a journal for each other, and sit in the coffee shop and write a brief inscription to each other in the front cover of the journal.

And now, you are ready to design a great relationship for yourselves.

If you are single, there is tremendous value in going through this process on your own. It will help to clarify what you are looking for and what is important to you. A great many people spend years in a difficult relationship and wish they had asked some of these soul-searching questions. Our society often treats singleness like a disease. You should not feel incomplete or deficient because you are single. Our single years are a great opportunity to develop an intimacy with ourselves, which is invaluable later on in our quest to develop a great intimacy with another. Being single is the chance we need to get to know ourselves.

Step 1: Establish a Common Goal.

If you are able to agree that your essential purpose as individuals is to become the-best-version-of-yourselves, then it should be relatively easy to establish that the common purpose and goal of your relationships is to assist each other in that quest. If you are unable to agree that your essential purpose is to become the-best-version-of-yourselves, then that in itself is worthy of a discussion. This discussion should focus on what you believe your essential purpose to be. From there you should move on to establish a clear and common goal for your relationship.

Step 2: Clearly Define What Makes a Relationship Great

Working from your earlier notes, discuss what you each believe to be the essential components of a great relationship. Drawing the best from each of your notes, pull together a brief and cohesive description of what a great relationship between you would look like. In many ways, this is a mission statement for your primary relationship. If done properly, this can be very powerful tool that will help clarify decisions and enable you to remain focused as the weeks and months pass.

Step 3: Agree on a Plan to Establish a Great Relationship

It is important that your plan be both realistic and measurable. For example, don't make "We will never argue again" part of your action plan. It is unrealistic and may run contrary to your essential purpose and mission statement.

It is also too vague and general to say, "We will be more loving toward each other." Your action plan must be measurable. At the end of each day, week, month, and year, you must be able to assess objectively whether you have honored the plan you are now creating.

Create an action plan. Try not to make it too extensive or complex; remember, you can come back to it once a month for refinement, and once a year for an overhaul if that's needed. Once you have created the plan, it is important that you both enthusiastically agree on it.

Before moving on to step number four, take a few moments to review each part of your action plan in relation to your commonly agreed-upon purpose and mission statement in order to make sure you are not contradicting your purpose and mission.

Step 4: Check to Be Sure That Your Plan Is Realistic

If our plan is simple stargazing, then our attempt to rejuvenate, restore, or simply improve our relationship is likely to be very short-lived. Take some time to review the first three steps and ask the following questions: Is the common purpose you agreed upon in step number one realistic? Is the mission statement you co-authored in step number two realistic? Is each step of your action plan realistic? By "realistic" I mean enough of a challenge to stretch you and encourage your relationship to grow, but not so difficult as to discourage you.

If you sense that you have far to go in your relationship from where you are to the great relationship you each want to have, it is important to break the journey down into manageable baby steps.

Step 5: Believe You Can Achieve Your Plan

Belief is a habit of the mind and spirit that is fostered by hope. When we begin to doubt our relationship, our thoughts tend to turn to the negative experiences of the past or the qualities that we find annoying in our partner. Hope for the future and belief in the plan you have enthusiastically agreed upon are fostered by forming the habit of turning your thoughts to the wonderful moments you have shared in the past and the qualities that you most love and admire about your significant other.

If you spend your days and weeks thinking about the negative aspects of your relationship and your partner, you will lose hope and you will stop believing. If you spend the empty moments of your day thinking about the wonderful memories you have created together and the qualities you love and admire most in your partner, your hope will grow and so will your belief that you can build a richer and more abundant future together.

Choose to believe.

Step 6: Make It an Absolute Must to Be Part of a Great Relationship

Discuss the things that are important to you and ask your significant other to do the same. The list may include career, friends, family, primary relationship, watching football with your mates, eating at great restaurants, having nice clothes, taking annual vacations, being financially secure, feeling appreciated, being healthy, or having a fantastic family home. The list would certainly not be limited to these, but they will give you a starting point.

Make a list of all the things that are important to you. Nothing is too small or trivial. Share your list with each other in its entirety. Then assign a rank of 1, 2, or 3 to each item on your list, with 1 signifying the things most important to you and 3 the things that are least important.

I am going to assume that your primary relationship made the list, and that it was ranked 1. What else did you give this highest ranking to? Ask yourself whether your primary relationship is more important than each of these.

In most cases you will be able to agree that your primary relationship is more important than anything else in your life. In your everyday life, however, you may put your work, your financial security, and any number of less important matters ahead of your significant relationship.

This exercise is designed to help you realize what is important to you and to your significant other, and to point out that when you reflect on it your primary relationship is the most important reality in your life. This exercise is also designed to help us learn to hold each other accountable. Next time you (or your partner) puts something of lesser importance ahead of your relationship, the other is responsible for gently reminding you of your priorities. At times circumstances will force something else to take priority, and these times call for acceptance and understanding. But these instances should be the exception to the rule, and not a way of life.

Imagine that your significant other died suddenly tomorrow; how would your life change?

Having realized that, apart from maintaining our personal integrity, nothing is more important than our primary relationship, we can now commit to making it a *must* to have a great relationship.

Step 7: Persevere and Follow Through

One way to prepare for a storm is to see it coming. Reviewing again your common purpose, your mission statement, and your action plan, what do you think is most likely to stop you as a couple and as individuals from following through with your plan? Write down what you think those obstacles will be.

Another way to ensure perseverance and follow-through is to schedule regular review sessions. Get out your planners right now: schedule a weekend away together in one year. Write the date in your journals. Then agree to meet to discuss your progress once a week for the next four weeks, and then once a month for the next eleven months. Schedule next week's meeting now.

Why is it that the very basic success skills that we employ in our everyday lives we often disregard when it comes to our relationships?

The final way to increase your chances of following through on your plan is to review it every day. You may decide to use your journal as your dream book also. Either way, read it every day. As it becomes more and more dense with dreams and goals and plans, you may only be able to read a couple of pages each day. But constantly be reviewing your plan to establish a great relationship. This will keep it fresh in your mind when your life is full of distractions.

The secret to following through and transforming our action plan into a fresh and vibrant relationship is to review the plan regularly (individually and as a couple), to have open, honest, and regular conversations about our progress, and to set some time apart once a year to revisit, refresh, and revise the plan.

Step 8: Hold Each Other Accountable to Your Purpose and Plan

The hardest part in all of this, at least in the early stages, may be summoning the courage to hold each other accountable to your commonly agreed-upon purpose and plan. It is important that we learn to do this in ways that are devoid of ego and filled with a genuine love for the other person. This love expresses itself in a desire to see those we love become the-best-version-of-themselves. If our partner sees our holding them accountable as a manipulative tool that we use to get our own way, then the response is likely to be resentment. If our partner genuinely feels that we are acting selflessly and out of a sincere desire to help him or her become his or her best self, then the response is likely to be much more appreciative and enthusiastic.

We should never try to hold someone accountable when we are angry, in front of other people, or for any reason other than the good of the relationship. It may also be important to remember that we are all human. We have good days and bad days; we have days when we are very energetic in the pursuit of our purpose, and days when we are not so energetic. Holding someone accountable requires that we learn when to challenge and when to encourage, when to confront a situation and when to simply let it pass.

We all need to be held accountable, but no one likes to have someone breathing down our necks every minute of every day. Done properly, holding your partner accountable will only encourage him or her to love and respect you more. Done in the wrong way, it will elicit resentment. If your partner responds with resentment, ask how he or she would like you to approach these situations.

Step 9: Don't Give Up in the Face of Major Challenges

A tree with strong roots can weather any storm. Your commonly agreed-upon purpose, mission statement, and plan provide the first deep roots. Regularly discussing your progress will strengthen these roots.

The storm is coming. In his best-selling work *The Road Less Traveled*, M. Scott Peck's now famous opening words were "Life is difficult." Many of us never accept this and as a result we never learn to thrive. Instead we are plagued by a discontent that is poisonous to the human experience. It is our misguided expectations that produce this poison. We encounter the same discontent and misguided expectations in many relationships. Many people enter into relationships expecting them to be blissful, to take away their loneliness forever, and to be ever fresh and exciting. These people are, of course, always disappointed.

Relationships are difficult. The reason is that these difficulties provide us opportunities we need to become the-best-version-of-ourselves. Life is difficult for the same reason. Learn to see every circumstance as an opportunity to become your best self, and you will master the art of loving and the joy of being loved.

Sooner or later, your relationship is going to find itself stared in the face by a major obstacle. If you stay together long enough, you may encounter a number of these major obstacles. Don't give up when they come along. Stay focused on your purpose, revise your plan if necessary, and press on.

Step 10: Get Quality Coaching

Think about getting some coaching. If you have never been to couples counseling, give it a try. You don't have to go forever. If you don't have any particular problems that you need to work through, just ask your counselor to teach you some techniques to improve your communication skills. Take your journals with you so you can share with the counselor the journey you are on together.

Get great coaching by listening to audio books and programs while you drive. On the first day of each month for the next twelve months, go to your bookstore and pick out an audio book about relationships. If you're not thinking about your relationships, they are not improving. The books will teach you to make a habit of thinking about the well-being of your relationships, and your relationships will improve simply by virtue of the mental attention.

At least once a year, go to a retreat, workshop, or seminar about relationships. There is nothing like stepping back from the day-to-day busyness of your life and while considering new and exciting ways to improve and refine your primary relationship.

Most important, start looking for two or three great couples that you and your significant other can spend time with. These couples will serve as friends, guides, mentors, and coaches. You will be able to practice many of the things you learn from them, and in time others will learn them from you and your partner.

Get quality coaching. Great coaches can make all the difference.

A PLAN MAKES ALL THE DIFFERENCE

What happens to businesses that don't have a plan? They fail. What happens to football teams that don't have a plan? They lose. What happens to relationships that don't have a plan? They begin to stagnate, fail, and die.

In almost every area of human life, a plan can make all the difference; this is particularly true when it comes to relationships. What's your plan?

I often ask readers to stop reading and write something down; less than 10 percent actually do. The other 90 percent say they either don't need to, will do it later, or can't be bothered. The 10 percent who do stop reading and write down their responses have a life-altering experience—not because of anything they read in my book, but because of what they wrote. I hope you will be part of the 10 percent. I hope you will take the time to answer the questions that have been discussed in this chapter and to formulate a plan for the continued growth and development of your primary relationship.

I am not suggesting that you have to plan out every tiny aspect of your future together; that would simply be scheduling. Planning is dreaming and goal setting that allows us to direct our energies toward the passionate fulfillment of a goal worthy of our lives and our relationship.

People who have great relationships don't have them because of chance or luck, but because they have a plan and they work the plan. It isn't enough just to work hard at your relationship. Some people work hard their whole life but never get ahead financially. Why? Usually it is not because of lack of talent or opportunity, but because they never had a plan.

Those who fail to plan can plan to fail. Most people are not planning to fail at their relationships, they are simply failing to plan . . . and as a result, relationships are failing all around us. One of the most powerful ways to show your love and commitment to a person is to make time to dream a vision of the future together. Can you plan all the details of that future? No. But the sheer act of dreaming and planning will consciously and subconsciously cause you to move more and more boldly in the direction of your richly imagined future. Tell the one that you love that you would like to set aside some time soon to dream a little about the future, and I can all but guarantee that you will ignite an enthusiasm within that person. Let us press on with the words of Bonnie Jean Wasmund in mind: "People will forget what you said, people will forget what you did, but people will never forget how you made them feel."

CHAPTER SIXTEEN

༄

DON'T JUST HOPE . . .

COMPLETELY LOVED?

There is a great deal more to intimacy than the miracle of physical love. And while it is easy to become preoccupied with physical intimacy, and with sexual intimacy in particular, our journey through the seven levels of intimacy encourages us to look toward the horizon and expand our vision of intimacy, love, relationship, others, self, and indeed, life.

Intimacy is the most enchanting of adventures, at once both exhilarating and frightening.

This intimacy we have spoken so much of consists simply of closeness to yourself when you are enjoying solitude, and closeness to others when you are enjoying company. It consists of knowing and understanding ourselves and the people we love. When knowing and understanding evade us, intimacy consists simply in accepting ourselves and others for who we are and where we are in the journey, right now, today.

You and I, we are here to love and be loved. The highest expression of genuine self-love is to celebrate in each moment your best self. The greatest expression of love for others is to assist in any way possible their quest to become the-best-version-of-themselves. It is love that captures the imagination of humanity and has intrigued the hearts and minds of men and women since the beginning. As far back as we can reach into history, the most common theme in theater, literature, art, and music has been love. Our fascination with the subject is unrivaled in the human quest for knowledge and experience. In a very real and practical way, we already have everything within us that we need to create love in our lives and in the lives of those who cross our paths. There are a great many things that we do not know as individuals and as humans collectively, but we know how to love.

Let me ask you this: if you wanted to make your significant other feel completely loved, what would you do? Are you doing those things? If not, why not?

The greatest power we possess is our ability to make people feel loved, and yet it is among the least used of human abilities. We know how to love, we know how to put others before ourselves, we know how to bring happiness to the lives of other people, and when we focus on loving people, we have a certain glow; we feel better about ourselves and better about our lives.

Nothing energizes us like love. Love animates the human person. Love breathes life into us like nothing else. This is why love is the supreme good, the summum bonum: love enables and empowers us in the pursuit of our essential purpose more powerfully than anything else.

Love is the best beautician. When someone who is in love walks into the room, you can just tell that he or she is in love. The way he walks, the way she talks, the way he smiles, the sparkle in her eyes, the glow in his face, the way she holds herself—all say, "I am in love." Everything about a person in love announces, "Something wonderful is happening in my life." Isn't it time we feel back in love with life—the mystery, the wonder, the adventure?

Love is the only true currency in our often bankrupt world. In the end, love is all that matters, love is all that you can take with you, and love is all that cannot be taken from you.

What would it take to make your husband or your wife feel completely loved? Seek the answer to this question, and you will find an invitation to experience the depth of intimacy and the heights of all human experience.

I WISH I HAD KNOWN HIM BETTER

Less than two years ago, my father died after a long-drawn-out battle with the tyrant we call cancer. My father was an extraordinary man. Not that he invented something that changed the course of human history; no, he was extraordinary in the very ordinary things of life. As a husband and a father, as an employee and a friend, as a member of his local community and as a citizen of his nation. The world is richer, and a better place, because he lived.

Every day I think about him. I ponder what he would do if he were faced with decisions and situations I am faced with. There are times when I wish I could meet him for lunch and just talk. Sometimes when I am feeling sorry for myself, I become sad because he will never meet the woman I marry or know my children. They will never know him. There is so much of my life yet to be lived that I will not be able to share with him.

There is a memory that refuses to leave me. With my brothers, I am carrying his coffin from the church after his funeral. One thought etched itself in my mind at that moment. I thought to myself, I wish I had known him better.

There are just so many things that I wish I could talk to him about one more time, and I can see us both sitting in front of the TV . . .

I had a wonderful father and a wonderful relationship with him. He made it a priority to make memories with me, and I treasure those now that he is gone. But he *is* gone, and I wish I knew more about his childhood, more about his parents, more about how he found his way when he was young. I wish I knew how he felt about things we never thought to discuss. I often wonder whether he held some knowledge that would help me further understand my path and the life I am being called to live.

All of this is just a young man who misses his father. But his dying has taught me one last lesson: take the time to get to know the people you love, deeply, for one day they will no longer be there, and when that day comes we will all wish we had known them better.

DON'T JUST HOPE . . .

Peter was an ordinary guy. He liked to watch football, drink beer, and hang out with his friends. From time to time, when he was alone, he would get a little introspective and start to think about where his life was going. It was then that he thought about relationships; more specifically he would wonder whether he would ever have a truly great relationship. He always concluded that he hoped one day he would.

One thing Peter loved to do was people-watch, and if you like people-watching there is perhaps no better place than an airport.

A few years ago, he was standing at the airport in San Francisco waiting for a friend when he had one of those life-changing experiences you sometimes hear people talk about . . . the kind that sneaks up on you when you least expect it.

Straining to locate a friend among the deplaning passengers, Peter noticed a man walking toward him carrying two small bags. The man stopped right next to Peter to greet his waiting family.

First he motioned to his younger son, who was perhaps five or six years old. Putting down his bags, he took the boy in his arms and gave him a long loving hug, and as they drew apart long enough to look at each other, Peter overheard the father say, "It's so good to see you, son. I've missed you so much."

The boy smiled shyly, averted his eyes and replied, "Me too, Dad."

Standing up, the man gazed deep into his elder son's eyes (the boy was maybe nine or ten years old) and, cupping the boy's chin with his hand, he said, "You're already such a fine young man, Nathan, I love you very much." With that he took the boy in his arms and gave him a long tender hug.

While all this was happening a baby girl was eyeing her father and squirming excitedly in her mother's arms, never once taking her eyes off the wonderful sight of her returning father. The man turned to the child now and said, "Hi, baby girl!" as he gently took her from her mother's arms, kissed her face all over, and pulled her to his chest, rocking her from side to side. The little girl instantly laid her head on his shoulder, motionless in pure contentment.

After several long moments he handed his daughter to his elder son, declared, "I've saved the best for last," and proceeded to kiss and embrace his wife. After a long moment, they drew back to look at each other. He stared into her eyes for several seconds and then silently mouthed, "I love you so much."

As they stood staring into each other's eyes, holding hands with both hands and covered in smiles, they reminded Peter of newlyweds, though he knew from the ages of their children that they couldn't possibly be.

All of a sudden, Peter became awkwardly aware of how engrossed he had become in this wonderful display of unconditional love, no more than an arm's length from him. In that moment he began to feel uncomfortable, as if he had intruded on something sacred. But he was amazed to hear his own voice asking, "How long have you been married?"

"Been together fourteen years, married for twelve," the stranger replied without breaking his gaze from his lovely wife's face.

"How long have you been away?" Peter asked.

The stranger turned to him now, smiled, and said, "Two whole days."

Peter was stunned. He had guessed, from the intensity of their greeting, that the man had been gone weeks, if not months. Two whole days, he thought to himself, and smiled. Now embarrassed, hoping to end his intrusion with some semblance of grace, Peter offhandedly said, "I hope my marriage is that passionate after twelve years!"

Suddenly the man stopped smiling. He looked straight into Peter's eyes with a forcefulness that burned straight through to his soul, and he said something that left Peter a different man:

"Don't just hope, friend, decide!"

And with that, the stranger picked up his bags and he and his family strolled off.

Peter was still watching them disappear into the distance when his friend came up to him and said, "Whatcha looking at?"

Peter smiled and, without hesitating, replied, "My future."

Great relationships don't come to those who hope for them. Hope is worthless unless coupled with real effort. Great relationships belong to those who decide to put in the effort and make them a priority. Don't just hope . . . decide!

Whether you received *The Seven Levels of Intimacy* as a gift, borrowed it from a friend, or purchased it yourself, we're glad you read it. We think you will agree that Matthew Kelly is a most refreshing voice, and we hope you will share this book and his thoughts with your family and friends.

If you are interested in writing to the author, wish to receive his free newsletter, *The Beacon,* would like information about his speaking engagements, or would like to invite him to speak at an event you are hosting, please address all correspondence to:

The Matthew Kelly Foundation
2330 Kemper Lane
Cincinnati, OH 45206
Phone: 1-513-221-7700
Fax: 1-513-221-7710
e-mail: info@matthewkelly.org
www.matthewkelly.org

ABOUT THE AUTHOR

Ơ﹏ﾟ

From amidst a culture preoccupied with speed, noise, and activity, has emerged a young man with a unique vision of life and a tireless passion for sharing that vision. Dynamic, and extraordinarily engaging, Kelly comes to the aid of a generation searching for some meaning in life beyond the pursuit of pleasure and possessions.

MATTHEW KELLY was born in Sydney, Australia, and over the past decade more than two million people in fifty countries have attended his talks and seminars. Against the backdrop of his travel to fifty countries, millions more have been touched by his writings and appearances on radio and television programs.

Both as a speaker and as an author, Kelly possesses a powerful ability to combine the ageless tool of storytelling with a profound understanding of today's culture and the common yearnings of the human heart. As a result, he captures our imaginations and helps us to see the challenges and opportunities of our everyday lives in a new light. With a keen sense of humor and heartwarming charm, Kelly seems to effortlessly elevate and energize people to pursue the highest values of the human spirit and become "the-best-version-of-themselves."